Academic
Anxiety

Allen J. Ottens, Ph.D.

ROSEN PUBLISHING GROUP, INC./NEW YORK

Published in 1984, 1991 by The Rosen Publishing Group, Inc.
29 East 21st Street, New York, NY 10010

Copyright 1984, 1991 by Allen J. Ottens

REVISED EDITION 1991

Library of Congress Cataloging-in-Publication Data

Ottens, Allen J.
  Coping with academic anxiety.
    1. Test anxiety.   2. College students—Psychology.
3. Stress (Psychology) 4. Academic achievement.
I. Title.
LB3060.6.O87   1984   378'.198   83-23108
ISBN 0-8239-1337-6

Manufactured in the United States of America

This book is dedicated to the memory of my parents, John and Doris, whose struggle with adversity taught me a whole lot about coping.

ABOUT THE AUTHOR ⬦

Allen J. Ottens received his doctorate in counseling psychology from the University of Illinois. He was formerly assistant professor in the Department of Social and Preventive Medicine, University of Maryland School of Medicine, and staff psychologist in the Psychological Services Clinic, Cornell University. Presently he is staff psychologist, University Counseling Center, Villanova University.

Dr. Ottens is a licensed psychologist and a member of the American Psychological Association. He is the author of numerous papers that have appeared in such publications as the *Journal of Behavior Therapy and Experimental Psychiatry* and the *Personnel and Guidance Journal.*

Contents

CHAPTER 1

Is Academic Anxiety
a Problem for You?

Introduction

This book is about academic anxiety; there are other equivalent terms such as test anxiety or evaluation anxiety, but I prefer the term academic anxiety. I think it better connotes the apprehension one feels about the overall picture of academic evaluation, including test-taking, test preparation, assignment completion, and so forth. Psychologists disagree somewhat about the precise definition of academic or test anxiety, but this theoretical issue needn't deter us. For now, let the term academic anxiety refer to disruptive thought patterns and physiological responses and behaviors that follow from concern about the possibility of an unacceptably poor performance on an academic task. Don't worry if that sounds complex, because we'll learn more later about the nature of academic anxiety.

Why Such a Book?

Above all, this book was written because academic anxiety, however defined, is a significant problem affecting a substantial number of students. Many colleges and universities offer counseling or special workshops to anxious students, and the demand for these services has probably never been so great as it is today. Further underscoring the significance of the problem is the fact that it has attracted the serious research attention of many counselors and psychologists over the past thirty years.

Although there is a well-established body of self-help literature aimed at improving the *mechanics* of studying— how to develop better study habits, note-taking skills, and so on—I believe there is an overdue need to focus on the emotional side of academics. I find it unfortunate that not much is taught in school about managing emotions. Most students probably understand mathematical theory better than their own feelings. I am repeatedly reminded of this by my counseling contacts with students who seem to be riding "emotional roller coasters," experiencing alternative highs and lows but not knowing why they feel so good one day and so anxious or depressed the next.

For the past half dozen years I have worked at the psychological clinic of a large university and have had an opportunity to see the problem up close and how students are affected. Of course, some students claim that getting "uptight" about a test or assignment helps to boost their performance. Up to a point that is true. A little anxiety (arousal) is beneficial in that it helps to orient and ready us for the task at hand. But too often the anxiety becomes excessive, and then students find their performance to be negatively affected. For some, the problem involves psychological distress in a particular course or subject area with the result that studying is done inefficiently (due to task avoidance or worry or both) and test scores do not reflect how much the student really knows. For others, the problem is more than decreased efficiency: academic anxiety may pervade a student's life to the point where he or she experiences almost constant dread about school, finds academic work unbearably distasteful, and scarcely enjoys campus social activities.

Finally, there is a different mood on campuses these days, probably associated with current social and economic uncertainty. Attractive jobs and professional school slots are in short supply, and old rules such as "A college education is a ticket to success" no longer apply. One response to uncertainty is to buckle down and get serious. In this regard, one Big Ten university administrator, after recently surveying the campus scene, has remarked: "These students are far less frivolous. They are less joyous."[1] This seriousness has spawned a growing conservatism that seems to be making it more acceptable nowadays to be keenly competitive for those diminishing opportunities. Of course, another response to uncertainty is to become anxious, to become so fretful about the future that one loses touch with oneself in the present. I think that there are better responses than deadly seriousness, cut-throat competitiveness, and blinding anxiety, and we shall explore some of them.

Is Academic Anxiety a Problem For You?

Perhaps the answer is already obvious to you. You may have received counseling or have considered counseling. Maybe you have been aware of signs that indicate some-

[1] *Time*, pp. 56 and 57, June 28, 1982.

thing is wrong: undue apprehension about studying, "freezing" during exams, and the like. But if you are not sure, scan the following checklist to see if any of these problems, which can be indicative of academic anxiety, are relevant to your situation.

Do You: . . .

1. keep reminding yourself while studying about the terrible consequences of a less than comprehensive understanding of the subject matter?

2. believe that practically all your classmates are more knowledgeable, less error-prone, or better prepared than yourself?

3. call to mind previous tests or study situations in which you performed below expectations and expect future situations to end as disastrously?

4. get upset with yourself after a test for having made a "stupid" mistake?

5. find that panicky thoughts, worries, or extraneous ideas repeatedly frustrate your efforts to concentrate?

6. impress on yourself again and again the importance of getting a good grade on a test or assignment?

7. find that remembering past successes fails to boost your confidence?

8. escape from important studying by performing irrelevant tasks?

9. attend to how other students are faring during a test?

10. find that no matter how much time you devote to studies you never feel well enough prepared?

11. worry that during an exam you may lose emotional control and "freeze up"?

12. engage in a lot of clock-watching during exams?
13. experience trembling hands or physical weakness during a test?
14. fail to ask questions of friends or instructors for fear of embarrassing yourself?
15. repeatedly resort to makeup exams or time extensions for assignments?
16. feel compelled to redo answers on homework or tests?
17. rush through test questions so quickly that you misinterpret directions or fail to notice important information?
18. experience physical reactions such as sweating, muscle tightness, or stomach distress that disrupt your effectiveness?
19. study too meticulously, such as trying to memorize almost everything or underlining virtually every sentence in the textbook?
20. get so flustered during an exam that you forget information you actually knew?

Reducing those twenty items to their bare essentials leaves four interrelated characteristics symptomatic of the academically anxious. I've seen these characteristics manifested over and over in students I've counseled. I'll sketch them only briefly now, but see if they describe any of your problems.

1. *Patterns of anxiety-engendering mental activity.* Counseling requires me to understand a student's personal experience. As students disclose to me their thoughts, perceptions, and notions regarding their academic difficulties, it's not hard to understand why they are so tense, because it's the sort of

thinking hazardous to anyone's mental health. A few examples will give you an idea of the troublesome mental activity I'm talking about. First and foremost is *worry*. Students trap themselves into insecurity by fretting over almost anything that could go wrong. Second, academically anxious students engage in a maladaptive *"self-dialogue."* We all carry on conversations with ourselves throughout the day, a stream-of-consciousness dialogue that includes self-reminders, self-directives, self-congratulations, and the like. But the inner speech of the academically anxious student is often punctuated by harsh self-criticism, self-blame, and panicky self-talk that produces anxious feelings and contributes to low self-confidence and disorganized problem-solving. A third example of this characteristic is the cockeyed *meanings and beliefs* students hold about themselves and their world. Students embrace erroneous beliefs about very important issues—how to define self-worth, how best to motivate oneself, how to cope with anxiety—and it is this sort of erroneous thinking that literally guarantees academic anxiety.

2. *Misdirected attention.* Another characteristic of academically anxious students is *misdirected attention.* This is a big problem area. Ideally, what is desired is full concentration on the academic task, whether it is reading a textbook, taking an exam, or solving a homework question. But anxious students let their attention become badly sidetracked. Attention can be diverted to *external* distractors (actions of other students, a clock, extraneous noises) or to *internal* distractors (worries, daydreams, physical reactions). Misdirected atten-

tion handicaps in two ways: first, if you let yourself become distracted, you simply can't work
efficiently; second, if you focus on worries or
personal concerns, you're going to become emotionally upset.

3. *Physiological distress*. Numerous bodily changes
are associated with anxiety—muscle tightness,
sweating, racing heart, and trembling hands,
to name several. Besides these bodily changes,
you're probably familiar with the emotional experience of anxiety, popularly described as a "sinking,"
"freezing," or "clutching" feeling. These physiological and emotional aspects of anxiety become
especially disruptive if interpreted as dangerous
or if they become an important focus of attention
during an academic task.

4. *Inappropriate behaviors*. If the three preceding
characteristics weren't bad enough, this last one
is a clincher. Repeatedly, academically anxious
students choose to act in ways that compound their
difficulties. I'm referring to behaviors that are
inappropriate to the academic situation. Avoidance
(procrastination) is common, as are withdrawing
prematurely from tasks and performing irrelevant
parallel functions (like conversing with a friend
while trying to study). The academically anxious
student also answers test questions in a rush or is
excessively meticulous in order to avoid a mistake.
Another incorrect action is trying to push yourself
when you're tense rather than taking a moment
to relax.

These are the characteristics or "symptoms" of academic
anxiety that we will work on controlling. If these charac-

teristics or checklist items describe experiences typical of your situation, this book could be of benefit to you.

Goals and Scope of the Book

The goals of this book are simple: to assist you to become a more effective studier and less frazzled test-taker. You might find, as an added bonus, that your grades will improve if you conscientiously apply these ideas and techniques. Of .course, grade improvement depends on a number of factors, such as the extent to which anxiety has been detracting from your performance, the difficulty of your coursework, and your motivation to tackle the work.

This book is not for those few students who are practically paralyzed by anxiety; rather it is suited for the student who functions at somewhat less than capacity due to inappropriate emotional reactions. You might use this book in conjunction with professional counseling, but I have prepared it primarily as a self-help guide. In that sense I've aimed it at an audience of one—*you*! I've endeavored to make concepts as understandable as possible and to use mostly nontechnical language, just as if I were talking to you as a client in an individual counseling session. Incidentally, I've drawn many of the ideas and observations from my counseling experience with scores of academically anxious students.

To help you gain more control over the emotional aspects of academics, later chapters cover in detail four broad content areas involving:

i. examining the nature of academic anxiety,
ii. developing a keen awareness of the characteristics relevant to your particular experience of anxiety,

iii. implementing a system for coping with academic anxiety,

iv. assisting you to acquire and apply a variety of corrective interventions to minimize the negative effect of academic anxiety.

Before going further, let me make a very important point: this book won't benefit you unless you take *responsible* action. That involves several things. First, read the chapters carefully and in consecutive order. I recommend that you read *slowly*—spend time with the book rather than cramming it down at one sitting. Devote time to mulling over the points presented, to rethinking your notions about academics, and to relating the information to your particular needs. Second, I suggest several exercises or "homework assignments" in later chapters. These are important and constitute a significant part of my counseling work with clients. I think you will find the homework interesting and little drain on your time. If you skip the exercises or perform them haphazardly, you could sabotage the effectiveness of the program. Finally, I urge you to *actively practice* and *experiment with* the anxiety-control procedures we will develop. "Actively practice" means that merely reading the book (a passive response) isn't sufficient. I recommend that you go beyond reading about new ideas and how to change behavior to the point where you act on the ideas and actually perform the new behaviors. By "experiment with" I mean trying out the anxiety-control procedures to see what works for you. Experimenting also implies creativity on your part. I can only make broad suggestions regarding certain procedures, but it's your job to tailor them to fit your unique situation.

Some Special Considerations

Sometimes difficulties with tests and with studying are not due to academic anxiety but arise from other causes. Thus, students may exhibit some of the checklist anxiety characteristics, but other problems are really at the root of their academic malfunctioning. Some case examples will illustrate what I mean.

Gwen's high school work demanded little of her, and she coasted through with decent grades. But the faster pace and greater responsibilities of college made apparent her deficient study skills. She needed much more time to complete reading assignments because of poor comprehension. Her class notes were fragmented and of little use for study purposes. She had other problems such as not knowing how to budget time effectively or how to write a research paper. Because deficient study skills held her back, other problems cropped up. Gwen started to compare herself unfavorably to classmates and to blame herself for her shortcomings. Also, because she did not have the time to prepare adequately for exams, she walked into tests in a highly vulnerable condition that led her to become panicky and fretful. Gwen's debilitating emotionality while studying and taking tests was an outgrowth of her deficient study tools. Her soundest first course of action is to seek remedial assistance from a learning skills specialist at her school. However, should her emotional distress persist after study skills remediation, measures would need to be taken to help her deal with what would then have evolved into a problem of academic anxiety.

Mike, a freshman in architecture, was earning barely passing grades. Because of his precarious academic standing, he reported an almost constant state of apprehension about schoolwork. The low grades were not due to a lack of effort; he applied himself conscientiously, went to all classes, and took a tutor. The problem was Mike's limited ability to perceive spatial relations. He had enormous difficulty envisioning how the same design might appear from top, side, or cut-away views. This perceptual dysfunction was a serious handicap in an architecture curriculum. It was not feasible to expect that massed practice or extra effort would soon bring Mike's spatial perception ability up to the level of even the average architecture student. For Mike, testing and counseling were recommended to help him find a more suitable course of study.

Janet was a junior laboring under a difficult pre-med curriculum that she detested. Frankly, she chose pre-med for wrong reasons such as stiff parental pressure and the money and good life offered by a medical career. She translated her dislike for her demanding courses into avoiding studying until the very last minute and then into poor concentration when she did pick up a book. As her grades declined and she became a less attractive medical school candidate, she was preoccupied by worries of what the future might bring: "What kind of job can I get with just a bachelor's degree in biology?" "Should I leave school for awhile to 'get my head on straight'?" In Janet's case, career and academic advising and personal counseling are indicated to help her deal with these confusing issues.

Bob had dated Kathy for a year when, abruptly, she ended their relationship. This breakup hit Bob hard, and he became quite despondent. He spent much time reflecting on the broken romance, seeking advice from friends, and planning how to win back Kathy's affection. During this period, the amount of time and energy Bob devoted to his work declined drastically. The resulting low grades fed his feelings of depression, causing him to call more into question his self-worth and self-confidence. Soon Bob felt overmatched by his academic responsibilities—he could not simultaneously keep pace with work and handle the emotional distress caused by the shattered relationship. Assignments and tests turned into ordeals that only reflected the helplessness he felt about his personal situation. Because of Bob's despondency and deteriorating coping capacity, individual psychotherapy was recommended as the treatment of choice.

These cases point out that other problems such as deficient study skills, limited ability, inadequate preparation, inappropriate choice of curriculum, and personal problems can bring about many of the symptoms of academic anxiety. The problems encountered in these case examples will require assistance different from that offered through this book. On occasion, the symptoms may persist even after the precipitating cause has been rectified, as, for example, in Gwen's case when she remained very apprehensive about studies even after remedial help had brought her study skills up to par. Then it became necessary to treat her apprehension as an academic anxiety problem.

A Look Ahead

Chapter 2 presents a detailed case example. It's a composite of many of the typical experiences reported to me by students. Often the experience of academic anxiety seems confusing and disjointed, but out of this confusion it's possible to derive certain patterns of symptoms or characteristics that are common to or define the problem. Once identified, these characteristics can give us valuable clues for coping with anxiety. Chapters 3 through 7 contain in-depth discussions of these characteristics. We'll look at precisely what can go wrong for the academically anxious student, and I'll suggest practical coping techniques for dealing with each characteristic. Chapter 8 gives you an opportunity to pull together everything you've learned. I'll present a systematic approach for managing academic anxiety and a variety of examples to illustrate how the coping techniques can be applied. In Chapter 9 I'll offer some practical strategies for developing test-taking skills.

CHAPTER 2

Characteristics of Academically Anxious Students

Introduction

The students I see in counseling are all intelligent and sophisticated young adults, yet many are perplexed about their emotional overreaction to academics. In so many words, they complain: "I don't know what happens. I get so upset, but I don't know why." Understandably, anxiety is very confusing and unsettling. The best way to get a handle on the problem is to examine what *does* happen. To do this we'll use a case example of a hypothetical student named Brian. Although he's fictitious, his experiences are typical of academically anxious students. The purpose of the case example is to sift through the confusion and identify characteristics or symptoms that underlie the anxiety problem. This is valuable information, for once we know what needs to be corrected, we can make better-educated judgments as to how the corrections can be accomplished.

The Case of Brian

Brian is a second-semester freshman, majoring in preveterinary studies at a large state university. He is a bright student, having graduated in the top 20 percent of his high school class. His grades, test scores, and career interest patterns were such that he was encouraged by his high school counselor to pursue pre-vet studies. Actually, Brian was never in doubt about his choice of college major. For as long as he could remember, he had enthusiastically responded: "A vet!" when asked what he wanted to be later in life. It's somewhat surprising that he got stuck on vet medicine since he had no special background, such as growing up on a farm or having a relative who was a vet, that would favor (or rule against) this choice. If forced to give reasons for his vocational aspiration, Brian answers that he thinks he would like working with animals and that vet medicine would be a way to channel his interest in biology into an esteemed profession.

There is another reason why Brian is enrolled as a pre-vet, and it's a reason of which he is only vaguely aware. Because he has for so long indicated to friends and family his desire to become a veterinarian, Brian believes that switching career plans would ruin the image others have of him. He imagines that to others he's not "just Brian" but "Brian the aspiring vet." Thus, he feels obligated to this choice because he thinks people expect him to carry it through. Moreover, if a veterinary career should not work out, Brian fears that friends might consider him a "washout" and that family would be disappointed by his failure to realize his potential. But the choice has proved to be a hard one for Brian, and not just because his science courses are so demanding. He has been on edge since September and hasn't relaxed into a comfortable student routine. The situation is psychologically demanding as well: much seems at stake, and a favorable outcome is uncertain.

Brian studied hard his first semester, earning a 3.40 average on a 4.0 scale. But this, he knew, wasn't good enough. He had heard horror stories about applying to vet school—how a large percentage of applicants are rejected, some who have almost straight As! As Brian surveyed his remaining years of college, he told himself that there would be little room for error.

Neither test-taking nor test preparation had posed problems for Brian in high school, but problems have surfaced during freshman year. Brian has been experiencing a lot of worry and apprehension several days before exams, and he feels a nagging insecurity about how much he knows compared to classmates. Studying has not been performed as effectively as before, with Brian finding that he requires more time and effort to complete assignments because much energy is wasted on worry. Then, on a couple of recent exams, Brian experienced the frightening sensation of momentarily "going blank," and he is concerned that on upcoming exams this problem could grow more serious.

The focal point of this case example is the semester's second physics test. Brian earned a B in first-semester physics, one of his least favorite courses. To make his academic transcript appear more attractive, Brian believes that he must earn an A this term. But on the semester's first physics test, he scored below the class mean. Fortunately, he may drop the lowest of his three midterm test scores, so this low score may not have to count toward his final grade. But that presents a problem: Brian feels he must exert more pressure on himself to do well on exam #2 since he will already have exercised his option to drop one low score.

Five days before the test, Brian drew up an ambitious study schedule calling for sixteen hours of review. That seems a lot just for physics, but Brian believed it justified since the test was so crucial. There was another less obvious reason for so much preparation: somewhere Brian had lost his "internal compass"—his sense of being able to gauge how much time a study task should take. Instead, Brian had been confusing his own needs with extraneous variables—should he overstudy in order to be a step ahead of everybody else? Should be overlearn the material to be on the safe side?

During those five days, Brian's psychological arousal kept peaking to the point where it was interfering with his review. Several little things contributed to his becoming overwrought. He would frequently remind himself of the test's importance and repeat to himself such commands as: "You've *got* to do well on it!" or "You've got to really *nail* this exam!" One way or another, he kept the importance of the test and the urgency of the situation foremost in his mind. He even developed a little habit of trying to predict the range of grades he might earn in all his semester's courses and then calculating all the resulting grade point averages. The margins of his classnotes were full of these calculations.

On the night before the test, Brian went to the library for his final reviewing, but it did not proceed smoothly. He was beset by a barrage of concerns and worries . . .

"What if I get another low test score?"

"What if I go totally blank tomorrow?"

"Time's running out and I'm still not finished reviewing!"

"Why am I always so worried? Why can't I concentrate better? What's wrong with me anyway?"

by swirls of unsettling mental images . . .

seeing in his mind's eye a mound of work piling up from other courses that have been neglected because of physics

picturing the returned physics exam, full of ugly red corrections and topped by an embarrassingly low total score

and by other lapses of attention . . .

thinking about what he might do over spring vacation

expressing his digust with the physics subject matter ("I hate this stuff! I just hate it!")

attending to his nervously churning stomach (and becoming worried about it)

glancing up from his book each time a female student passed through his section of the library.

Even under the best of circumstances, the physics is very difficult since it involves complex theoretical material, but because Brian labored under the additional handicaps of worry and interfering emotional arousal, the task became an ordeal. After about three hours in the library, Brian had performed only intermittent studying. As his panic increased, he exhorted himself to "Calm down!" and "Pull yourself together!", but by then these self-orienting directives proved too little, too late. At that point, Brian figured there was no sense in frustrating himself further, and he returned to his dorm.

On the morning of the test, Brian and other early arrivers milled about in front of the closed doors to the lecture auditorium. He spied a student named Beth who was doing some furious last-minute cramming. Beth's style was to catastrophize about exams and to downplay her ability, but she usually scored among the highest on tests. He could hear her complaining to friends: "I still don't understand how to derive Coulomb's Law from Gauss's Law. I guess if there's a question on that, I'll have to punt." Her comment struck Brian as ominous, as he remarked to himself: "If Miss Know-It-All is stuck, what does that say about me?" He could feel a growing sense of apprehension and tenseness.

When the doors opened, Brian took his assigned test seat. He soon discovered that he was sitting on the "wrong" side of the auditorium: examinations were being distributed first to students across the room. Although no one was allowed to start before all tests were out, this rule was routinely ignored. Brian glanced at students already busily at work. His stomach began to churn, and to Brian it seemed like a rumbling that could register on the Richter scale. "Hurry up with those exams!" he almost blurted. "I'm already in a hole!"

With the exam finally in hand, Brian attacked the first question. He worked diligently for about five minutes and arrived at an answer, but it looked intuitively wrong. It *was* wrong! In his haste to get started, he had misread the question and had used an inappropriate formula to solve it. Now he was further behind, and he hadn't even attempted the harder questions. He sensed an almost instantaneous swell of emotionality. This was a danger sign: not only had he wasted precious time but now his emotions were coming unglued. Almost automatically, Brian quickened his pace. He leafed frantically through the test trying to estimate the difficulty of the remaining questions, at the same time admonishing himself for causing this setback: "You screwed up . . . how can you be so stupid?"

After thrashing through the test, he decided his best strategy would be to work a problem he knew he could answer, so he returned to question one. While reworking this question, he noticed a disconcerting split of attention—now *onto* the test (crossing out incorrect steps from the old answer, deriving data from the given information, plugging the new data into the right formula), now *away* from the test (worrying about falling further behind, attending to his nervous stomach, noting that other students were already on page two).

Once Brian had completed the first question and had obtained a reasonable answer, he felt a little safer. He took a deep breath and plunged on. With question two, his thoughts centered mainly on manipulating numbers and concepts into the right configuration. As his attention became more task-focused, he eventually settled into a comfortable pace and managed to finish without further incident.

Brian considered himself lucky to have salvaged most of the situation. But there was no denying that his studying had been no picnic and that the first ten minutes of the test had been fraught with panic and doubt. He was not sure why he had escaped; he just hoped these problems wouldn't occur on his next test.

Despite the confusion, complexity, and apparent uniqueness of the case example, it's possible to extract from it a number of commonalities between Brian and other academically anxious students. What is characteristic about these students that seems to assure an anxious reaction? Where and how do their situations break down? It is important to know exactly what goes wrong and where problems occur because that gives us valuable clues for correcting the situation and for managing anxiety. The next section will initiate the process of developing your awareness of the specific characteristics associated with academic anxiety. In Chapter 1, I introduced you to the first four interrelated characteristics; now our case example suggests three more. In later chapters each characteristic is thoroughly examined. Out of Brian's experience emerge the following characteristics that I commonly see manifested in academically anxious students:

i. misdirected attention
ii. patterns of anxiety-engendering mental activity
iii. physiological and emotional distress
iv. inappropriate behaviors
v. ineffective or maladaptive coping choices
vi. negative interpretation of events
vii. special personal meanings attached to academics.

Misdirected Attention

Obviously, where you focus your attention is a key factor in successful studying and test-taking. This statement is borne out by research showing high-anxious students performing more poorly on evaluated tasks than low-anxious. In the words of psychologist Jeri Wine, " . . . the explanation for this performance difference lies in the different attentional focuses of high- and low-test-anxious persons in evaluative conditions, with the test-anxious individual dividing attention between self-preoccupied worry and task cues and the less anxious person focusing more fully on task-relevant variables."[1]

One striking aspect of the case example is the prevalence of misdirected attention, so characteristic of academically anxious students. But Brian's experience suggests that the problem of roving attention has some very sticky complications. Like other high-anxious students, Brian's attention seems almost irresistibly drawn to off-task distractors, *especially when confronted with an evaluated task.* Thus, when faced with an academic situation (like a "crucial" physics test) that involves the risks of grading and evaluation, attention is most likely to be misdirected. This seems paradoxical, because it is just during these situations that utmost concentration is desired. We saw how Brian, in the library and the testing room, let his attention flit to irrelevant internal and external distractors:

Internal	*External*
Daydreams about vacation	Female students walking through library
Worries about possible low test scores	Watching other students during exam
Preoccupied with nervous stomach	

(Take a few moments to go back to the case and identify several other examples of these distractors.)

---

[1] Wine, J.D. Cognitive-attentional theory of test anxiety. In. I.G. Sarason (ed), *Test anxiety: Theory, research, and application.* Hillsdale, N.J.: Lawrence Erlbaum, 1980, p. 355.

On the positive side, we saw that when Brian focused his attention almost exclusively upon the test, he was able to settle down and absorb himself in the work. This points out that the more successful you are in keeping attention on the task, the more likely you are to keep anxiety at a manageable level and to stay at peak efficiency. Not only is it important to know *where* your attention is focused, but also to know *when* you distract yourself, so that you can take swift action to direct yourself back on the task. I say swift, because the longer you dwell on worries or other distractors, the greater your chances of increasing anxiety and decreasing performance.

We'll delve more deeply into the topic of attention in Chapter 4, where I'll describe additional problems associated with misdirected attention and introduce you to some coping responses to help you stay more on-task.

I hope you tuned in to Brian's displays of toxic thoughts, mental images, and inner speech. As frantic, negative, and worrisome as I made it sound, *I doubt that it was dramatic enough* to be accurately characteristic of many students. By this I mean that I routinely hear my clients engage in biting self-criticism, utter expressions of hopelessness and futility, and entertain worries of every shade and hue. It is no wonder that these students feel anxious or complain of low self-confidence—I would, too, if I thought that way.

What kinds of anxiety-engendering mental activity do we find in the case of Brian? Actually, there are a number of different kinds, but I'll touch on just a couple for now:

Absolutistic thinking refers to a mental set that allows practically no flexibility or alternatives. Brian's pre-exam statement: "You've got to do well on it" is such an example. To this statement we could justifiably add the trailing clause: " . . . *or else it's curtains!*" Look at what Brian's thinking is doing to himself: first, he's demanding a rigid level of performance (he *must* "do well"); second, only a very narrow band of excellent grades are acceptable outcomes; and third, if one and two don't occur, the only result is his *academic death*. Absolutistic thinking puts Brian in a precarious position: since only narrow, inflexible outcomes are available, he increases personal risk, and when situations become riskier, he is more prone to worry.

Brian's unspoken command: "Hurry up with those exams" is an example of *panicky internal speech*, which both reflects and feeds back into the panic he experienced. The problem with panicky internal speech is that it aggravates one's feeling of helplessness.

At this point, review the case example. Identify other examples of absolutistic thinking and panicky internal speech. What other hazardous mental activity do you notice? How similarly does this thinking style reflect your own?

At least three important points can be derived from the case example that address the academic anxiety problems of all students. First, what you say to youself and what you think about are factors in initiating and maintaining anxious arousal. Second, I think you see the value in "cleaning up" this toxic thinking and internal speech. Finally, the case example gives us a clue for managing academic anxiety: if it is possible to think ourselves into an anxious state, and if the "wrong" kind of thinking can interfere with our performance, then perhaps the "right" kind of thinking can help us keep anxiety at a manageable level and increase our effectiveness.

In Chapter 5 I present a comprehensive array of anxiety-engendering thinking (many examples of which are verbatim student statements from actual counseling sessions), and I discuss, suggest, and invite you to experiment with a variety of alternative thinking styles.

Physiological and Emotional Distress

This characteristic consists of the *emotional* experience of academic anxiety (variously described as feeling panicked or "frozen") and the *physiological* arousal (perspiration, rapid heartbeat, coldness of hands and feet, gastrointestinal upset, muscle tightness) caused by activation of the sympathetic division of the autonomic nervous system. Let's again examine Brian's experience for some general insights into this characteristic of academic anxiety.

You may recall Brian's surge of emotionality following his incorrect answer to the first physics question. At that point his approach to the test crumbled into disorganization: his thinking went awry (note the self-criticism) and his behavior became ineffectual (rapid thrashing through the exam paper). Moreover, he interpreted the presence of this emotionality as a danger sign, a sign that his emotions were poised to unravel. Recall, also, Brian's efforts to reduce his emotional arousal after three frustrating hours in the library. His self-commands to "calm down," though well intentioned, were too late to be effective against his rather advanced stage of panic. These three aspects—disorganization of thinking and behavior, negative interpretation of emotional arousal, and belated efforts to curb arousal—are common examples of what can go wrong with regard to the experience of emotionality.

Brian's most prominent physiological symptom was a "nervous" stomach. How can his reaction to stomach distress become a problem? Recall that as Brian was waiting for his exam paper, he felt a churning sensation and then *overestimated* its intensity (rumblings of "earthquake proportions"). This tendency to exaggerate the actual intensity of physiological symptoms is typical of the academically anxious. Once the symptom intensity has been overestimated, a problem arises: one is then more likely to keep part of one's attention tuned to the symptom, and in this way it interferes with performance. Other problems result from inappropriate coping or responding to the physiological experience of academic anxiety, and these are explored in Chapter 6.

Understanding the types of problems associated with this characteristic of academic anxiety gives us clues for coping. For example, to combat disorganized thinking and behavior arising from high levels of emotionality, we want a coping response to direct us back on task. To keep emotionality and physiological symptoms from getting too advanced, we want to apply coping responses earlier rather than later; one such coping response is a method of relaxation that is incompatible with being tense. Finally, the case example cautions us about negatively interpreting, overestimating, and too closely attending to emotional and physiological arousal; hence, coping requires more adaptive ways of thinking about and talking to ourselves about this arousal, as well as redirecting attention on task. We will develop and try out these coping responses in Chapter 6.

Inappropriate Behaviors

In his haste to start the test, Brian misread the first question. He had so sensitized himself to the urgency of the situation that, in his accelerating state of panic, he rushed pell mell through the question. Moreover, if I showed you a videotape of Brian during the test, you'd notice that he *looked* nervous; his overt (observable) behaviors would give him away as the "anxious one." The case example suggests that *panicky behaviors*, such as those exhibited by Brian, reduce performance effectiveness, reflect a panicked state, and feed into a sense of helplessness and disorganization. There are several other kinds of inappropriate behaviors that are characteristic of academically anxious students. Chapter 7 discusses these.

Knowing that inappropriate behaviors represent a problem area, what can be done to manage or overcome them? In this regard, increasing self-awareness is of prime value. It's important to keep a third eye, so to speak, on your overt behavior. You can subsequently use awareness of any inappropriate behavior as a signal or cue to apply more adaptive alternative actions. What these might be, how to adapt them for yourself, and suggestions for creatively applying them are also included in Chapter 7.

Ineffective or Maladaptive Coping Choices

Misdirected attention, anxiety-engendering mental activity, inappropriate behaviors, and emotional and physiological distress—are there any more ways Brian can get himself into hot water? The answer is, unfortunately, yes. Let's examine the case in order to address another relevant question: what woeful methods does Brian choose to cope with a stressful situation or to manage anxiety? Three such methods are intimately associated with Brian's anxiety problem and are common to academically anxious students in general.

The "push harder" coping approach. Despite being acutely sensitized to the "critical" nature of his academic situation and despite feeling emotionally overwrought, Brian's choice of coping was to push himself harder. How so? Scheduling sixteen hours of study review was one, "over-psyching" himself ("You've got to do well") was another. Also revealing was Brian's coping style during the test: when faced with a wrong answer to question #1, his automatic reaction was to quicken his pace. Actually, the best way to cope is to slow down and take stock of the situation. Can you identify any other examples where pushing himself was Brian's preferred method of coping?

Ineffective calmatives.   Brian, as well as other academically anxious students, chooses well-intentioned but often ineffective methods to reduce emotional arousal. Brian's library review session illustrated this point. First, he waited far too long before initiating calmative measures. Second, his choice of measures—"Calm down!" and "Pull yourself together!"—are neither creative enough nor potent enough to be effective; they're just stereotyped phrases that carry little personal meaning. Third, I doubt that his calming phrases, barked out command-style, will have a soothing effect.

The "thanks-I-needed-that!" coping approach.   This coping style utilizes self-punitiveness or urgent reminders, like hard slaps across the face, in order to bring about alertness and motivation. Thus, when faced with a stressful situation, Brian's responses were: "You screwed up!"; "What's wrong with me?"; and "Time's running out!" This brand of self-talk is usually not helpful. Not only do those reminders contain little usable information, but they are poor motivators because they aggravate panic and feelings of futility.

If these habitual coping choices are so dysfunctional, why hang onto them? That question is taken up in Chapter 8. Also in 8 we shall develop a more adaptive approach for coping with academic anxiety. We'll incorporate the coping responses from the next five chapters into an organized system.

Negative Interpretation of Events

Brian's overhearing Beth's comment about deriving Coulomb's Law and assuming that this portended his downfall . . .

Brian's arriving at a wrong answer, experiencing emotional arousal, and then expecting to come unglued . . .

Brian's earning a 3.40 average and figuring that put him only a hop, skip, and jump away from "washing out" of pre-vet . . .

These three excerpts have one aspect in common: each illustrates how Brian negatively interprets potential setbacks, frustrating events, and mistakes. Instead of regarding them as situations that required a particular coping approach, Brian interpreted them as personal threats. I'm not saying that setbacks and mistakes are desirable or pleasant, but I want to point out that Brian tended to catastrophize (expect the worst) when they occurred.

Frequently, I find that when a student's academic progress seems blocked due to a mistake, he/she interprets this frustration as an indication of danger. Once that negative interpretation is made, the student experiences higher levels of anxiety and may not choose effective methods to cope. In this book we shall adopt the following approach: instead of signaling a time to start catastrophizing, the occurrence of a setback will set the stage for choosing effective coping responses. We shall have more to say about negative interpretations at various points in later chapters.

Special Personal Meanings

"What does being enrolled in pre-vet studies at State U. mean to you?" That's a tough question since it involves values, motives, and expectations. Ask Brian that question and he might give you a nice, socially acceptable answer like: "It means that I'll have the opportunity to ground myself in the sciences so that I'll stand a better chance of making a successful application to vet school." This is Brian's *explicit* meaning of higher education—explicit in the sense that it is the clearly defined, generally agreed upon purpose for being at State U. But there are other, hidden meanings attached to college and pre-vet studies that are not so directly expressed or accurately identified. These are called *implicit* meanings.

What are some special, implicit meanings that Brian attaches to academics? We've seen a couple. Brian's feeling obligated to a vet career because he publicly committed himself to it is one such meaning. To renege on or fail to achieve this goal might cause people to think poorly of him. Second, not performing up to his full potential, Brian believes, will cause family to feel let down. Thus, there's more at stake than getting well grounded in the sciences: a self-image must be secured and others' feelings must be protected. As Brian lets academics become imbued with extraordinary meaning, the work becomes harder—there are more issues to worry about and points of vulnerability.

Examples of some of these meanings, their effect, and alternative ways of thinking are the gist of Chapter 3.

In conclusion, although this chapter touched on the characteristics of academic anxiety, it provided an overview of the scope of academic anxiety, a problem that ranges all the ways from where attention is focused at the moment to the meanings attached to an entire college career. I think you see, too, at this early stage how these seven characteristics are interrelated—behaviors are tied in with thought, attention with physiological distress, and so forth. This chapter was intended to help you develop a feel for those things that can go wrong and for the nature of academic anxiety. The next chapters will probe these issues more deeply and provide specific coping responses and a system for managing academic anxiety.

CHAPTER 3

Special Meanings That Make Academics More Threatening

Introduction

I f going to college involved nothing but learning more about political science or becoming more proficient at mathematics—if taking or studying for a test were nothing but an exercise in displaying knowledge of chemical reactions or matching wits with the French professor, academics would be taken closer to their "face value." That is, the coursework would be difficult but not much harder than the inherent nature of the subject matter itself. But, as we saw in Chapter 2, special meanings or concerns become attached to academics so that a great deal more currency is added to evaluative tasks. What are some of those special meanings? Psychologist Donald Meichenbaum[1] noted several: (1) concern over loss of control and fear of being overwhelmed by anxiety; (2) concern to gain the esteem of authority figures or peers or both; (3) concern that high academic achievement might jeopardize social relationships with members of the opposite sex; (4) concern for job success or entry into graduate school; (5) concern by a male that academic failure would result in being subject to the military draft. A few others that come to mind include: (6) a student's strong desire to emulate the academic or career success of an older sibling; (7) academics viewed as compensation for low athletic ability; (8) concern that inadequate performance might confirm character deficiencies (e.g., prove to the student that he or she "doesn't have what it takes"). Obviously, given students' various backgrounds and experiences, there could be a limitless number of such concerns. Most, however, can be subsumed under four general types of special meanings. Identifying these four general meanings, detailing the problems inherent in each, and devising alternative ways of thinking is one topic area covered in this chapter.

These meanings and concerns not only add more significance to academic tasks but also cause the situation to become fraught with greater risk and uncertainty. Of course, when a task or situation is viewed as being harder and riskier, anxiety is a likely by-product. In a very real

---

[1] Meichenbaum, D., and Butler, L. Toward a conceptual model for the treatment of test anxiety: Implications for research and treatment. In I.G. Sarason (ed.), *Test anxiety: Theory, research, and applications.* Hillsdale, N.J.: Lawrence Erlbaum, 1980, p. 198.

sense, these meanings can be said to underlie academic anxiety.

How do I mean "underlie anxiety"? For academically anxious students, these meanings and concerns are known by another name: *worry*. Look over the above eight examples of meanings. Notice that each represents a focus of concern over which a student could do much serious worrying. Worry is a prime anxiety-engendering mental activity. Anxiety-engendering mental activity is one of the characteristics that appear to define the experience of academic anxiety. We shall see, too, how academically anxious students use worry as a maladaptive coping choice (another characteristic). Thus, our second main topic area of Chapter 3 includes a close inspection of worry, the purposes it serves, and how situations can be viewed in less worrisome ways, thereby saving psychological wear and tear.

Those Low-Down, Mind-Messin', Special Meaning Blues

We have seen that students pin high hopes on successful academic achievement. Because of the plans that seem to hang in the balance, academic evaluation takes on enormous personal significance. Concerns abound that goals or plans may go haywire: Will grades be good enough to maintain a scholarship? Can satisfactory progress be made toward one's degree? Can one be competitive for the right graduate or professional school? Must marriage be postponed because of academic troubles? Can one avoid the awful possibility of summer school makeup? Will future happiness be spoiled? These concerns can be summed up in *Special Meaning #1: If the academic situation is seen leading to an unfavorable outcome, then cherished plans may not be realized, and that would be terrible.* Once this conclusion ("that would be terrible") has been made, the academic situation takes on elements of psychological risk and personal threat. Anxiety results, as manifested by the worries that occur when fretting over the possibility of foiled plans.

In order to feel more secure and less troubled by academic anxiety, it is necessary to divest Special Meaning #1 of some of its power. While it is true that some plans may not materialize, must their nonoccurrence be interpreted as "terrible"? If we "de-terrible-ize" alternative outcomes, perhaps they can be viewed as less fearsome or upsetting. Furthermore, instead of worrying or catastrophizing about undesired outcomes, perhaps there are more appropriate coping responses whereby losses can be minimized. We shall discuss how to return some of that power to yourself so you feel less at the mercy of the vagaries of the situation and less impotent in the face of undesired outcomes. What can be done, after and before the fact, to reduce feelings of threat and increase one's sense of power and control? Let's begin by examining two students' experiences.

Laura* was a client of mine several years ago. When I first met her she wasn't eating, cried most of the day, and had some suicidal thoughts. She was confronted with what she termed a "personal crisis." Despite conscientious study efforts, she was being clearly overmatched by demanding pre-med course work. As she accumulated more and more unacceptably low grades in organic chemistry and biology, she felt her plans for a medical career slipping away. It was when she decided it was fruitless to stay in pre-med that

* Not her real name. Details about her background and those of other students have been altered to conceal their identities.

the crisis struck. "Almost two years of work is down the drain," She told me. "Look at the time and money I've wasted. I'm a has-been at twenty." Laura had never considered any option other than medical school, and now she was faced with abandoning that choice. But not long after her acute crisis period had passed, she initiated steps to deal with her shifting academic direction. She knew that she wished to remain in a health-related profession, and career information and academic advising helped her to select nursing as a strong alternative. Gradually she came to interpret the nursing alternative less as a symbol of personal tragedy than as an acceptable way to apply helping skills, use her mind creatively, and be personally independent—all factors she related to her sense of happiness. She later transferred to another college and received a bachelor of nursing degree. There she was such a dedicated and committed student that she eventually earned a master's. Today she teaches in the nursing program of a medical school and has more career responsibility and challenge than many M.D.s.

Keith, a computer science junior, came to my office with a pressing concern. His final exam in a computer course was only seven days away, and he needed to pass this test convincingly in order to pass the course. What complicated the matter was Keith's spotty academic record. His department warned him that if he failed one more computer course, he would be expelled. With so much riding on this one exam, Keith felt such pressure that he was not concentrating adequately to study for it. He felt powerless to deal with such an unthinkable outcome as expulsion. "What am I going to do? What if I fail? What if I can't get into another college?" were the worries he turned over in his mind. I suggested to him some before-the-fact maneuvers which, though difficult to perform, might provide him with a larger margin of safety. I urged Keith to meet with the professor of the computer science course and apprise him of the situation. Specifically, this involved Keith's explaining the department's ultimatum, disclosing his difficulty with concentration, and asking for the professor's advice. To Keith's surprise, the professor was understanding and offered him an option of an individual oral exam if the written test score was insufficient. Keith was relieved, since he claimed he could better communicate his knowledge of the subject orally. Given this understanding and flexibility, Keith prepared for and passed the test without incident.

Laura and Keith faced situations where much was at stake and alternatives looked bleak, but they managed nonetheless. Their experiences suggest several specific points about what can be done to feel less trapped by circumstances, how to "de-terrible-ize" the crisis, and what steps are helpful for coping.

First, don't underestimate your coping skills. Even if the worst happened, you would, in all likelihood, scramble to make the best of the situation. I'm reminded of an older client who was "unable" to drive beyond the city limits lest her car suffer a mechanical breakdown and strand her miles from a garage. "Suppose, for a minute, that the worst does happen," I asked her, "and your car breaks down fifty miles from town. Whatever would you do?" She winced and looked perplexed but after a short pause collected her thoughts and replied: "I guess that after a while I'd venture out of the car and walk down the road to some farmhouse. I'd use the farmer's phone to call a mechanic to tow me to the service station. It would be expensive, but what else can one do?" Note that even with a "terrible" outcome like a breakdown, steps can be taken to cope with the problem. In fact, viewed this way, such outcomes become inconvenient, undesirable, or expensive instead of terrible, and an inconvenient or expensive situation is usually easier to deal with than a catastrophic one. We saw with Laura that when a crisis ocurred, she sought out information and alternatives. The amazing thing about us humans is that when one avenue is blocked we seem to have the capacity to adjust.

Second, academic evaluation is rarely an all-or-nothing phenomenon. Although a low test score or grade may seem like an indelible stigma on one's record, seldom does one such mark cause anything approaching academic disaster. Ask friends or relatives if their personal or professional lives were ruined by a terrible grade. Usually they report that even if low grades necessitated a switch in plans, they adjusted to the change and that, all things considered, life turned out agreeably well. Even less than hoped for scores on the dreaded, "if-you-blow-it-you're-finished" Medical College Admissions test need not comprise your epitaph. This point was impressed upon me during a luncheon with admissions officers of two of this country's most prestigious medical schools. As these administrators discussed desirable attributes of applicants, it was clear that they conscientiously strove to evaluate the whole candidate. No reliance was placed on any fixed score or grade. Certainly, if evaluation is viewed in rigid pass/fail, make/break terms, academic tasks take on a forbidding quality because of the risk of seemingly ruinous consequences. The truth is that there is more flexibility in the academic system than perhaps is realized. You may occasionally run into a hardliner or unapproachable Ivory Tower type, but if you have a legitimate concern, instructors, as Keith discovered, are often helpful and reasonable. Opportunities for makeup work, special considerations, and second chances abound.

Third, anchor yourself in the here-and-now. When

academically anxious students encounter frustrations or potentially devastating situations, they tend to emit expressions of hopelessness and futility and catastrophization. Laura's statements (e.g., "I'm a has-been at twenty") are prime examples of expressions of hopelessness—a prediction of an end to her chances for future happiness. Keith's catastrophizations (e.g., "What if I fail?") are tantamount to rehearsing for tragedy. Catastrophizations are based on a "What if . . . ?" sentence contruction in which the blank can be filled in with the disaster of your choice. This construction is especially risky because "What if . . . ?" worries are easily interpreted to portend personal threat. Besides evoking feelings of terribleness and powerlessness, expressions of hopelessness/futility and catastrophization present another problem: a future-tense orientation. I'm not saying that planning for the future isn't important, but it is very easy to be waylaid by future concerns, especially when the emphasis is on predicting the worst and rehearsing for every conceivable setback. To reduce feelings of powerlessness and the terribleness of the situation, it is important to determine what specific steps need to be taken now in order to cope. Laura's and Keith's situations became more manageable as they focused on present-tense tactics such as seeking career information and meeting with the professor. Instead of dwelling on how terribly things might turn out, the key is making behavioral *adjustments at the moment*.

Many people have a fascination with making wide-ranging assumptions about their personalities from tidbits of information. For example, your favorite color or zodiac sign supposedly signifies that you possess particular traits and preferences. Likewise, it may seem reasonable to assume that test scores tell us more about ourselves than just our degree of familiarity with a certain academic discipline. What tends to happen is that students utilize disparate bits of information about their ability level, evaluation outcomes, and "goodness" of performance to rate themselves as persons and to make profound (and often dubious) assumptions about their personality characteristics. We've spoken about how academically anxious students feel that their careers are at stake, and now *Special Meaning #2* compounds the problem by causing students to feel that their "selves" are on the line as well.

Special Meaning #2 is as follows: *If one's performance, evaluation outcome, or ability level is less than acceptable (however defined), then one is less acceptable as a person. In other words, one's self-worth is intimately intertwined with one's performance.* Students who embrace Special Meaning #2 set themselves up for the ultimate undesirable outcome, namely self-rejection. Through this meaning, students impart an unhealthy kind of significance to academics. In effect, they are saying: "A good grade means I'm O.K." But if a good grade isn't forthcoming, then this signifies something is wrong with them as persons or with their character. Then the interpretations are: "That means I'm lazy" or "I'm a failure" or "I'm inadequate." In the course of counseling students, I've heard several say: "If I fail, I'll never be able to look at myself in the mirror!" I think you can appreciate the fact that this type of thinking and a relaxed, confident approach to academic work are incompatible.

The idea that personal worth equates with superior performance or high ability level or both is deeply ingrained in our society. It's so ingrained that we hardly question the momentous assumptions we make about selfhood and personality traits on the basis of adequacy of performance. For example, our favorite baseball team loses a first-place lead, and we brand the players as chokers and bums or worse because their performance wasn't good enough. We observe behavioral outcomes and automatically use that information to rate people and ourselves as good or bad. Advertisers capitalize on this idea. You've seen this scenario a thousand times: a woman bemoans the fact that because she can't get her laundry perfectly clean her family must appear in public in telltale gray clothing. We are given the message that the imperfect laundry implies a careless, thoughtless, objectionable woman—serious assumptions to make based on such a trivial aspect of life. Somehow it may seem logical that if one loses ball games, launders improperly, or lacks certain abilities, then one, as a person, rates as lazy, no good, incompetent, or dumb; and by letting the adequacy of performance reflect personal worth, we arrive at identities like these:

Mediocre job = mediocre person
Halfhearted attempt = lazy person
Less than superior performance = not having what it
    takes

This type of thinking is especially prominent in our educational system. From the earliest moment of elementary school, children compare artwork and arithemetic problems, and it soon becomes clear whose work looks best and is best received and whose doesn't measure up. As the bright pupils receive all the accolades, the others are left with the question: "What's wrong with me?" Not only do these children come to think of themselves as less worthy, but they hardly ever hear a significant other provide a counterargument to that assumption. Our collective thinking on this issue is so cockeyed that we believe the brightest *deserve* more attention, affection, respect, and consideration than those less gifted. Moreover, most of us believe that those of greatest intelligence (or anyone who possesses high levels of almost any socially valued trait or ability) are naturally happier or more self-fulfilled. But is it true that an Einstein's or a Beethoven's view or experience of the world is any more correct, meaningful, or satisfying than our own?

If students buy into a system that equates self-worth with performance, in which rewards are parceled out discriminately, and in which the gifted are considered richer and more deserving, it is very likely that they will put a premium on perfection and striving to do their best. Unfortunately, this often leads to immobilization. Witness the perfectionist or overachieving student who exhaustively researches every term paper and overstudies for every quiz. He or she exerts enormous energy to avoid any unacceptable evaluation that might mean relegation to the ranks of the mediocre. If a bad mark can be construed to signify a character or cognitive deficit (lack of intelligence, lack of what it takes), then this student will overwork to avoid that stigma.

Perfectionism also operates in reverse by fostering procrastination. If, for example, a research paper must be done perfectly, the task of writing it therefore becomes more difficult. Once a task becomes harder, it stands a greater chance of being avoided. However, sometimes procrastination is its own reward: it's psychologically easier to signify a character or cognitive deficit (lack of intelligence, lack of time) than to lack of ability, which has so many negative self-implications.

The mistaken notion that adequacy of performance and ability level connect with self-worth is one of the most difficult concepts for students to reconceptualize. Perhaps an example will illustrate the kind of rethinking needed to break that connection. I've included an excerpt from a therapy session conducted by psychologist Arnold Lazarus. Dr. Lazarus' client is a young man who experienced great difficulty speaking in public because he felt he would become personally unworthy if he performed poorly. The excerpt begins with Dr. Lazarus responding to his client's challenge: what if you were banned from the practice of psychology?

CLIENT   Well, let me ask you the same thing. Suppose you were banned from practicing psychotherapy and from teaching psychology. I mean how would you feel?

THERAPIST   Are you implying that the loss of your job would be identical to my being expelled from the fields of psychology and psychotherapy?

CLIENT   No, I realize that you have invested far more time and effort and all that into your career, but what I'm driving at is that you would be more than "inconvenienced" if you had to find a new way of earning a living.

THERAPIST   Sure, it would be extremely inconvenient and very disruptive, but hardly catastrophic.

CLIENT   Oh, come now!

THERAPIST   Here's the crucial factor. Are you listening? I want you to hear this very clearly. I am not a psychotherapist, I am a person who practices psychotherapy. Suppose I'm kicked out of psychology and I'm looking around for another career and a new source of income. I study, take some exams, and end up teaching high school English.

CLIENT And now you have less income and less status and less prestige. You would probably sell your house and move into a less expensive neighborhood...

THERAPIST But I can envision myself still being reasonably happy and fulfilled despite adopting a different modus vivendi. I am still the same person, the same husband, father, friend, brother...

CLIENT You might lose some so-called friends.

THERAPIST And I might gain others.

CLIENT But I wonder how many people really like us for ourselves?

THERAPIST Is there such an entity as a "self"? What does it mean to be "liked for one's self"? I suppose that there are certain continuities in behavior that let us make predictions about our responses and other people's reactions in different situations, but we are still talking about behavior. If people like me for "myself" it means that they value or respect the way I behave at various times and across different situations.

CLIENT That's my point! No matter what situation you are in you are always responded to by others as Dr. Lazarus. But if you had to eke out a living in trying to teach kids how to punctuate sentences, a lot of people might decide that you are no longer worth having over for dinner—if you see what I mean.

THERAPIST So what you seem to be saying is that in your own life situation you cannot really see yourself adjusting to an entirely different life-style.

CLIENT Wait a minute. Please answer my question first. How would you feel about being dropped by many people who are presently your social circle?

THERAPIST My friends get a lot more from me than my professional expertise. Some of my acquaintances might drop me, but they would be replaced by other casual contacts. And this is not true across the board. The people who play tennis with me are not interested in my occupation. The people with whom I play cards, enjoy music, go bowling, or boating would not reject me. My wife and children would not desert me . . .

CLIENT How can you be so sure? Perhaps your wife might stick it out, but she would doubtless let you know about her basic resentment in other ways.

THERAPIST So I have to actively practice psychotherapy in order to maintain the love of my wife, the caring of my children, the respect of my friends. According to you, my occupation is at the core of my very existence. No wonder you become so anxious when speaking in public. Your whole being is under the gun. If you give a poor performance, everything can be threatened. It's not merely your job that is on trial, but as you stand before the audience you are on trial as an employee, a husband, a friend, as a total person. If someone warned me that the next time I gave a public talk I would lose everything—job, home, friends, family, self-respect—unless I gave a sterling performance, I too would be anxious.[2]

Special Meaning #3 is: *If one's academic standing or performance isn't up to par, then one risks losing the esteem, respect, or approval of important people.* The problems posed by Special Meaning #3 are varied, but some sketches can illustrate how it makes academic life tougher.

Edwin began law school with some lofty ideals. He had thought that after graduation he might work for a legal aid service or citizen advocacy group. Failing that, he thought it would be nice to return to his small hometown and establish a comfortable law practice. However, he was not in law school long before he let himself get caught up in his classmates' crush for grades, class ranking, and law review competition. With practically everyone vying for positions with prestigious firms, it seemed obligatory for Edwin to do the same, though it never really felt right for him. Eventually he abandoned his original plans to champion underdog causes, began to grind away at

[2] From Arnold A. Lazarus, "Toward an Egoless State of Being." In Albert Ellis and Russell Grieger (eds)., *Handbook of Rational-Emotive Therapy*, pp. 114–116. Copyright © 1977 by Springer Publishing Company, Inc., New York: Used by Permission.

the books, and joined the "paper chase." His motivation: a fear that classmates would not respect him if he, too, weren't shooting for a job with a top firm.

Edwin's situation reveals one of the problems inherent in Special Meaning #3, namely a *loss of personal power*. Notice how Edwin gave up his power in deference to others. First, he discounted and modified his original career preferences in order to curry others' favor. Next, he allowed himself to feel fearful lest classmates hold unfavorable opinions of him. Finally, by aiming for only a certain kind of legal position, Edwin restricted his range of career choices and hence his degree of personal freedom.

Marc's parents were financing his education. Since they controlled the pursestrings, they insisted that Marc apply himself to his studies, and his earning Dean's List honors was their standard of satisfactory academic achievement. As Marc struggled to maintain parental approval, he complained bitterly to friends about this unfair treatment. He could have achieved some financial independence by joining ROTC or taking a part-time job, but he didn't because his parents wouldn't have approved.

Besides giving up his power totally to parents, Marc is also running into the problem of *conditional acceptance*. Being dependent upon others for approval raises the risk of conditional acceptance, meaning that Marc is O.K. as long as he acts the way people want, but if he deviates from their standard, they threaten to pull out support.

The freshman rhetoric instructor announces an assignment that involves writing a brief paper comparing two short stories. About a dozen hands go up. "Is this supposed to be a *research* paper, or can it be mainly my own ideas?" one students asks. "Can I contrast the stories instead of comparing them?" asks a second. "How long is the paper supposed to be?" "Handwritten or typed?" Question after question.

Seventeen students sit around a table in a political science seminar. Not a controversial word is ever spoken; in fact, hardly anyone says a word period. The professor remarks to a colleague: "They sit there like lumps, looking at each other to see who dares speak. I crave class participation—just let them say something!"

Julie practically memorizes her class notes so she can regurgitate them back to her teachers on tests. Since she earns exceptional grades, her system seems to be working.

These three sketches point out how Special Meaning #3 *curtails creativity and spontaneity.* If you operate under this meaning, you'll try to . . .

make sure what you do has full prior approval—never plunge ahead without first checking it out thoroughly;

aim to please, even if it shortchanges your education;

exhibit such bland, uncontroversial behavior that no one could possibly take issue with it;

subscribe to the aphorism: "It is better to remain silent and be thought a fool than to speak and remove all doubt."

Carl, a senior accounting student, enrolled himself in a rugged advanced accounting elective. By performing over and above what was required, Carl hoped he could win favor with his advisor. Carl suffered through the course all semester without the professor's once commenting on Carl's supposed conscientiousness. In fact, unbeknownst to Carl, the professor thought he took the course simply because he wanted to.

Carl's attempt at approval-seeking through the process of *ingratiation* is a difficult maneuver, and not just because he got himself saddled with a tough course. Although he wanted to present himself positively to the professor, he had to be silent about his real approval-seeking motives and instead convey the impression that he took the course because of his thirst for knowledge. Since Carl could not be honest about his ingratiation tactic, he could only make a calculated and risky guess that it would be positively received. However, for the tactic to work, the professor had to be open to its influence, and since he read no special meaning into Carl's taking the course, he obviously wasn't open to such influence. Finally, ingratiation maneuvers like these may backfire: the professor might have interpreted the maneuver as "apple-polishing."

We got a taste of what Special Meaning #4 is about in Chapter 2 in Brian's case example. Recall that he put more pressure on himself to excel because he believed that not succeeding would cause his family deep disappointment. Specifically, Special Meaning #4 states: *If one's academic standing or performance isn't up to par, then significant others will have cause to be emotionally upset.* If #4 is true for you, you may be assuming an even greater academic burden and putting yourself at risk of experiencing anxiety.

It is an almost universal belief that our actions and ways

of being directly cause others to experience various emotions. We see this belief in operation all the time in daily life. For example, a husband snaps at his wife: "I wish you'd lose weight. When we're out in public, *your appearance embarrasses me!*" Or we might complain to someone: "Stop your pacing up and down. *It's making me nervous.*" Such thinking is also common in situations involving academic themes:

> A science teacher indignantly announces to his class that he's "disgusted" by their poor showing on a standardized advanced placement test.

> A student decides to leave a pharmacy curriculum for one in special education. She receives a phone call from her mother who remarks: "You know, your decision has bitterly disappointed your father."

> A good student intentionally muffs her performance so that fellow classmates won't feel so stupid in comparison.

Of course, there are other alternative explanations to these situations. The science teacher has such exacting standards for his class that *he sets himself up* to become upset when the standards aren't met. It is not the daughter's leaving pharmacy that disappoints father, but rather what father *tells himself* about the event.

There's a sort of magical quality to the belief that if you act in a particular way, then presto!, another individual will automatically feel a certain emotion. That is not true, because between any action and another's emotional response is that person's *interpretation* of the action. It is the interpretation that is responsible for how he or she feels. In a similar fashion, students may magically attribute their anxiousness to external influences such as a test, assignment, or professor. But that's not the way emotions arise. Instead, we submit each stimulus—event or action—to a complex interpretive process. Against each stimulus we bring to bear a sizeable amount of mental machinery: what we tell ourselves about the stimulus, how we appraise it, and what we remember from past situations are part of the interpretive process that determines whether we perceive the stimulus as amusing, fearsome, disgusting, or inconsequential. It is not so much the stimulus that elicits an emotional reaction as it is our interpretation of it and the personalized meaning we abstract from it.

It's tempting to think that we might possess such power over others that we can make them feel the gamut of emotions. But if you get caught in the trap of believing you have that control, the power struggle could be turned against you. That's called *emotional blackmail,* in which "victims" claim that your behavior is responsible for their bad feelings, with the purpose of subverting your intentions. The familiar plea of the jilted lover: "If you leave me, I'll be so depressed I'll kill myself," is a form of emotional blackmail. But please do not misunderstand me on one point: although you are not responsible for others' emotions, you do not have license to act irresponsibly. The impact of your behavior on others still must be taken into account. Thus, students who view college as a four-year joyride while parents honestly scrimp to finance this "education" are acting irresponsibly and having a negative effect on their family.

In this section we have laid out the main special meanings or concerns that add an extra factor of difficulty to work and that generate the specific themes over which students worry. The issue of worry is covered in the next section. It is my experience that to the extent these meanings become important parts of one's academic life and to the extent that more worries are subsequently generated, the likelihood increases that one will experience chronic academic anxiety. Of these four meanings, which is (are) most relevant to you? How, specifically, can you define the particular meanings you attach to academics? Take time to write them down and rethink them in light of this discussion. It will probably take some time to feel clearer of their influence, but as you divest yourself of these excess concerns, academics will become easier for you.

Worry

What sort of problems exist to worry about? For the academically anxious there's an almost infinite variety, but some common ones include:

> worrying about lack of time (e.g., approaching deadline, only a few minutes left on a test)

> worrying about being compelled to cheat if the exam is too hard

> worrying about receiving a poor grade or score

> worrying that one's pocket calculator will conk out during a test

> worrying about being caught off guard by a trick question

> worrying that failing a course will bump you off graduation sequence

> worrying that you'll come emotionally unglued while taking an exam

worrying that after all your test preparation, you won't be well enough prepared.

Most worries can be traced back to one or more of the four special meanings. Often the special meaning behind the worry may not be fully expressed, so the worry amounts to the tip of the iceberg of the greater underlying meaning or concern:

VERBALIZED WORRY:	"I won't have enough time"
UNSPOKEN MEANING:	So I'll probably do poorly and ruin my chances for a 3.0 average (which relates to Special Meaning #1)

VERBALIZED WORRY:	"I'll make some dumb error again . . . "
UNSPOKEN MEANING:	which further proves my basic inadequacy (Special Meaning #2)

VERBALIZED WORRY:	"If this turns out to be too hard, I'm worried I'll resort to cheating . . . " "and, if I'm caught, I'll risk being thought
UNSPOKEN MEANING:	of as a contemptible person (Special Meaning #3)

Since worry is a close companion of academically anxious students, an investigation into the phenomenon of worry is worth our while. The extraordinarily sophisticated mental capabilities of *Homo sapiens* allow for futuristic thinking—imagining, planning, preparing. This is a wonderful gift, if used properly. But just as we are capable of self-enhancing kinds of prognosticating, so, too, can we use this mental capacity for worry—fretful rumination about anything that could go wrong, which leads to an increase in perceived personal vulnerability and even greater dread of uncertainty. In a nutshell, that's what anxiety is all about. Because anxious students worry so much, they must assume that they derive benefit of some kind from it. After all, a behavior must provide some payoff, otherwise one wouldn't engage in it. Let's examine some common types of presumed payoffs for worry and fretful rumination. To many students, these payoffs appear at first glance to be considerable, but in reality they are only illusory.

Worry as a source of motivation. I frequently meet students who unquestioningly subscribe to the belief that worry is a good motivator. These students hold that if they conjure up images of impending catastrophes it will spur them on to work harder to prevent their occurrence. However, if worry were really such a good motivator, our world would be populated by a race of eager beavers. Sometimes worry does galvanize one into action, but often it is a poor motivational source, and its net motivational effect can be negative. Worrying tends to make a mildly aversive task or situation even more odious or fearsome. And when tasks or situations take on a threatening quality, we tend to avoid them. Rather than worrying, simple self-reminders that certain tasks require attention are usually sufficient.

Worry as proof of concern. Sometimes students operate out of a belief that can be expressed as follows: "If I worry a lot, that's good thing because it means I'm taking my work very seriously." Thus, worry may be reassuring in that its presence seems proof that one is a concerned student. There may be an additional payoff: the respect and admiration of others who are impressed by seriousness, worry, and mental anguish. However, this belief is clearly an example of dysfunctional thinking, because it is possible to be a concerned and ambitious student without worry.

Worry as preparation for emergency. "Worry is needed to help me prepare for any emergency or contingency. I've got to worry; otherwise I'll be caught unprepared." True or false? This is a belief that academically anxious students hang onto tenaciously. For many, ceasing to be worried about grades, unfinished work, and possible exam questions would mean being utterly defenseless. According to this belief, the worrying provides protection. "If I didn't worry," these students aver, "how could I prepare or rehearse for all of the possible things that could get screwed up?" Wrong on at least two counts! First, one could never get fortified against all the things that presumably could go wrong. Second, it is mistaken to assume that just by worrying about future events one will be better able to cope with them. Paradoxically, fretting causes so much tension that one becomes less capable of dealing with problems in the here and now. It is certainly beneficial to anticipate events so that proper preparatory steps can be taken, but to distress oneself about unpleasant events or consequences is superfluous and does not constitute a helpful coping tactic.

Worry as reason for success. Students occasionally argue that worry is valid and necessary: "I've got to worry," they say, "because if I stopped worrying, the roof would cave in on me." I can understand how difficult it is to abandon worry, especially since many students attribute their academic success to it. My contention is that we function successfully *in spite of*, not because of, worry. Letting go of worry can be risky business, in a sense, because you may believe that it has gotten you this far in your academic career. The truth is that worry has no positive effect what-soever on one's work and that it amounts to nothing but a nonproductive mental activity. However, if you do think that worry favorably influences your performance, that could qualify as superstitious thinking—much the same as believing that putting "body English" on a rolling bowling ball will bring down more pins.

Rather than yielding self-enhancing results, worry usually backfires. One problem is that there is a *snow-balling* quality to worry: worry begets worry. Academically anxious students commonly lament that although they begin a test or academic task feeling only moderately apprehensive, the anxiety builds and builds until it be-comes detrimental to performance. What is happening is that the student perceives more and more stimuli in increasingly threatening terms. Part of the reason for this escalating emotional arousal is that the anxiety is fed by a sequence of worries. For example, a student remarked: "Before the test started, I was worried that I'd get myself upset and nervous. Sure enough, ten minutes into the test I started to get a bit uptight, so I tried to relax for a few moments. I discovered that my attempt to relax wasn't very successful. When I realized I wasn't calming down, that really shook me. I became concerned that if I couldn't calm down from this level of anxiety, I'd really be in hot water. That's when I really began to worry about not get-ting any more nervous!" Notice how consideration of one worry, instead of producing problem resolution, sensitizes one to additional concerns that beg to be fretted over.

Another drawback is that worry acts as a kind of *cognitive interference*. When one is engaged in worrisome thinking, it is impossible to devote full attention to a task or test. Imagine all the different worries going on in an exam room—how the test will be curved, time running out, etc., etc.—all of which are incompatible with planful problem-solving, creative brainstorming, and efforts to recall information. Worry, then, interferes with precisely that kind of mental activity that benefits test performance.

If you check over the worries listed at the beginning of this section, you'll notice that each *dwells wholly on the negative.* This points out an additional disadvantage to worry. Although worries sensitize one to a myriad potential dangers, they offer little in the way of *positive* clues or directions for dealing effectively with a situation. Thus, I may fret about making a "dumb" computational error, but this worrying doesn't teach me how to minimize such errors or suggest ameliorative strategies if a mistake is detected.

Worry can interfere with performance during both the studying and test-taking phases of academic work. A goal is to reduce the frequency, intensity, and invasiveness of your worrying so that learning of subject matter is improved and so that worry does not hamper your recall and organization of information during an exam. Uncoming chapters, especially Chapter 5, illustrate several types of worrisome, panicky thinking and include a variety of coping responses that can be employed to counter the negative effects of worry common to both phases.

To conclude this chapter 1 shall present two coping responses that can be adapted to controlling worry specifically during the studying or test-preparation phase: *stimulus control of worrying* and *hyperbolic imagery.* Before detailing these coping responses, I should point out that I commonly hear students say that they "can't help it" when their thoughts seem to be automatically diverted onto worries or other distractors. There is no question that developing a new response to worrisome thinking requires patience and practice, but I believe that if you are conscientious you will reap the benefits of less painful and more productive studying.

Coping Response #1: Stimulus Control of Worrying

You've probably received countless times from friends or parents the advice "Don't worry!" From a practical side, this advice is almost useless, because it is virtually impossible to refrain completely from worrying. But, if we can't eradicate worrying, perhaps we can arrange it so that worry is restricted to its own place and time. This *stimulus control of worrying* is in marked contrast to what typically occurs during study sessions: students sit at their desks attempting to study, but their concentration is repeatedly inferfered with by bouts of worry and task-irrelevant reverie. The result is that worry and daydreaming interfere with studying and vice versa.

Stimulus control procedures strive to make your study station a place where only actual studying prevails and to restrict daydreaming and worry to their own time and location. The frequency and interfering quality of worrisome thinking should be thereby reduced. The following example illustrates the implementation of stimulus control procedures:

> Each time Rita sat at her desk to study, she was beset by a couple of worrisome themes. Her parents were close to a separation, and she worried about how this would affect the family. She was concerned, too, about finances for college and worried about how she could simultaneously manage academics and a part-time job. Furthermore, she spent a great deal of potential study time musing about her relationship with her boyfriend, Paul. Clearly Rita has some

personal issues that warrant time and attention, and she would be doing herself a disservice if she allowed studying to interfere with their careful consideration. Nor, on the other hand, do we want these personal issues to disrupt studying. In order to give both study time and worrying/daydreaming time their due, Rita set up a stimulus control procedure such that 45 straight minutes of every study hour would be spent at her desk in concentrated, task-focused studying. The remaining 15-minute block was to be spent in a straight-backed chair at the other side of the room and was reserved for uninterrupted attention to any or all of the following:

    i. irrational panicky thinking regarding her family or academic situation,
   ii. rational, planful thinking about coping with her particular stressors,
  iii. romantic daydreams about Paul.

If during the 45-minute study segment she became aware of any worry or daydream, she *simply acknowledged* this attentional lapse and reminded herself that such mental activity could be engaged in fully later at its appointed time and location.

I recommend several tips for arranging your own stimulus control system:

a. For each hour of anticipated study, reserve a 10- to 15-minute block for uninterrupted worry or reverie. (Some students argue that 10 to 15 minutes is too long to "waste" on nonproductive thinking when actually, for many students, the amount of nonproductive time *spent at their desks* far exceeds 10 to 15 minutes.)

b. Work consistently at a particular study station (carrel or desk) so that it becomes associated in your mind as a place where nothing but work is accomplished.

c. Choose a location for worrying/daydreaming that is both *distant* from the study station and somewhat *uncomfortable* (unheated hallway, hard chair, etc.).

d. If worrisome or other task-irrelevant thinking occurs during the study segment of the hour,
   i. simply acknowledge the fact that your attention has strayed,
   ii. remind yourself that later in the hour such task-irrelevant thinking will be freely allowed,
   iii. refocus your attention onto the task (Note: you may have to perform those three steps many times during a 45-minute study segment— that's to be expected; don't be too discouraged if your attention still wanders even though you've made numerous efforts to stay on task.).

e. During the 10- to 15-minute off-time, worry, plan, or daydream to your heart's desire.

f. *Practice* this coping response. After conscientious practice you should notice an increase in concentration and a reduction of interfering thoughts while studying. Remember to practice exactly as recommended. Any coping response can be sabotaged if you fail to implement it in the appropriate fashion.

g. Remember that the goal is to separate worry from work—each is to be performed in its own place at the appropriate time.

Coping Response #2: Hyperbolic Imagery

What often happens is that we entertain a worry or two (and several variations on them), but we rarely go any further beyond the worries than to merely regard their terribleness. As a result, the worries retain their power to elicit anxiety. One way to go beyond a worry is through disputation or counterargument, a coping response that is addressed in Chapter 5. Another response to worry is *hyperbolic imagery,* hyperbole meaning overstatement or exaggeration. Through hyperbolic imagery we can take a worry far beyond its threatening quality and exaggerate it to such an extent that it becomes absurd instead of fearsome. Hyperbolic imagery places the worry in a different perspective so that the illogic behind it stands out in sharp relief. This coping response is especially helpful with worries that we logically know are unlikely to occur but that we let run on in our consciousness, much to our vexation. Here's how it works:

Dave was in a tough curriculum but was managing to more than hold his own. However, he commented to me: "I know it's silly, but I keep plaguing myself with the worry that I'm going to flunk out." This was followed by another worry that he would thus be denied an opportunity for a personally fulfilling career. I suggested that Dave not stop with his usual catastrophizing but extend the worry through hyperbolic imagery in order to underscore its essential absurdity. In Dave's words is the elaboration on the worry that he visualized: "I'm worried that my courses next semester will prove so hard that I'll flunk or be forced to leave school. But I'm so caught up in worrying about next semester that I completely gum up all of my current courses. I see myself receiving a notice from the university that I am to be unconditionally expelled. The notice comes on a big pink slip and is personally delivered to my dorm room by the university president. He drags me by the neck out the door and down the main campus street. Hundreds of students line the street jeering me. I'm forced to wear a scarlet letter F. At the entrance gate to the university the president picks me up bodily and dropkicks me right up and over the gate. I soar high and far, and I finally land on a huge, greased metal slide—a slide that extends all the way from campus down to the Bowery. I slide and slide and end up deposited in a Bowery gutter. A couple of winos offer me a drink out of a bottle wrapped up in a paper bag. From there I go completely downhill. I see myself undergoing a total metamorphosis—tattered clothes, unshaven face, hollow eyes. But it's just the right appearance for my new profession, which is wiping car windshields for nickels that I use to buy cheap wine. And I see myself doing this for thirty years, all because I flunked out."

To develop your own hyperbolic images: take the worry far beyond its usual catastrophic level. Give your creativity free rein. Exaggerate the situation to show the worry in its absurd or ludicrous light. Use your own personally relevant images, employing Dave's example as a guide.

Conclusion

The issues examined in this chapter—personal meanings or concerns attached to academics and the role of worry—are at the core of academic anxiety. I hope you appreciate the degree to which they put one at greater risk of feeling anxious, overwhelmed, or vulnerable. Certainly, these meanings and worries increase the difficulty level of one's overall academic career and interfere with one's efforts to remain task-focused. I've urged you to identify the meanings you attach to your work and to rethink them in the light of our discussion. Also, I suggest that you employ coping responses #1 and #2 to reduce the deleterious effect of worry upon studying and test-preparation. In Chapter 4 we shall address another characteristic of academic anxiety, misdirected attention, which often poses problems of an urgent or immediate nature, especially during examinations.

Attentional Pitfalls

Introduction

In this chapter we shall investigate a fragile and evanescent academic factor—focus of attention. Whereas special personal meanings can remain relatively stable over time, focus of attention shifts back and forth, off-task and on, virtually unconsciously. Even the simple act of determining that one's attention is task-focused upsets concentration, just as the act of observation disturbs the true location of Heisenberg's "uncertain" electron. Obviously, attentional focus plays a key role in efficient studying and anxiety-management, but nowhere is its effect more keenly felt than during test-taking.

Academically anxious students are most likely to misdirect attention when difficult academic tasks are carried out under evaluative conditions; that is, when performance is to be graded or when some psychological investment is at stake in the task. Despite the fact that evaluative situations require sharp attention, we find instead that academically anxious students divide attention between on- and off-task stimuli. Consequently, performance effectiveness decreases; and worse, with attention focused on such internal distractors as worries or negative self-evaluations, students are more likely to go off-task under stressful conditions than less anxious students who seem to exert greater effort to be task-focused. However, when the test or task is performed under nonevaluative conditions with no strings attached, misdirected attention and anxious arousal do not present problems.

Years ago, psychologist Irwin Sarason observed that more-anxious and less-anxious research subjects (S's) differ with respect to their attentional focus under evaluative or stressful conditions. In Sarason's words:

> . . . S's scoring high and low in anxiety differ in the response tendencies activated by personally threatening conditions. Whereas low scoring S's may react to such conditions with increased effort and attention to the task at hand, *high scoring S's respond to threat with self-oriented, personalized response.*[1] (p. 405; emphasis added)

What are these "self-oriented, personalized responses" mentioned by Sarason? Where does attention get misdirected? How does misdirected attention prove a problem for academically anxious students? The next section addresses these questions. The last section of the chapter suggests coping responses for increasing task-focused attention during test-taking and studying.

Attentional Pitfalls

We noted in Chapter 2 that attention can be misdirected onto external or internal distractors. In this section we

---

[1] Sarason, I.G. Empirical findings and theoretical problems in the use of anxiety scales. *Psychological Bulletin*, 1960, 57, 403–415.

shall be more specific as to the form and subtance of these distractors.

External distractors refer to environmental sources of interference. Probably the most common environmental distractor is *noise*—ranging all the way from a neighbor's loud music to the gum-snapping of the person seated next to you at an exam. Certainly, noise conditions are not conducive to task-focused work, but the academically anxious student seems more susceptible to nuisance noises. This is true for several reasons. Since academically anxious students may not be as absorbed in their work, they are more likely to be sensitized to noise as a distraction. Also, noise can be a handy source to point to as a source of frustration when work is not going smoothly, and then students can feel justified in giving in to the "impossibility" of the situation.

Attention to social-evaluative cues represents another common category of external distractors. Frequently during a test or performance evaluation, the critical question for the academically anxious student becomes: "*How* am I doing?" rather than: "*What* am I doing?" In order to answer the former question, students scan their external environment, being vigilant or sensitive to cues that might provide feedback concerning the appropriateness or adequacy of their performance. For example:

Peggy was to give an oral report to her psychology class about stages of child development. However, she has a low regard for her effectiveness at oral presentations. She went into this particular presentation with the "mind-set" that her fellow students would think her report boring. As she delivered her report, she scanned her audience, searching for cues to corroborate her negative prediction: was anybody yawning? fidgeting? appearing somehow uninterested? She was more preoccupied by these distractors than she was by the information she was supposed to be presenting. If she did perceive a sign that might indicate disinterest, she interpreted it as a personal threat and let it feed back into her negative opinion of her ability. With each such negative interpretation of a cue, she felt more flustered, hurried herself to get through her talk (which resulted in a less coherent presentation that was more likely to be poorly received), and became increasingly attentive to subsequent audience cues.

Some students report feeling uncomfortable when a teacher paces the aisles while monitoring a test. These students are usually quite attentive to the teacher's comments or facial expression that could be interpreted as dissatisfaction with their performance.

Recall from Brian's case example (Chapter 2) that he focused his attention on other students during the physics test. By glancing over at their exam papers, Brian hoped to get some indication of his progress compared to that of his classmates.

A final example of an external distractor is the exam room clock. Again, the purpose of clockwatching is to assess how one is faring with regard to time. This is commonly reported as one of the most disruptive distractors, because diminishing time is so easily interpreted to mean that one's performance is in jeopardy.

Audience cues, teacher reactions, exam room clock—all are examples of external distractors which, if attended to excessively, present several problems:

    i. decreased performance efficiency,

   ii. each distractor is easily interpreted as signifying personal threat or risk,

  iii. once so interpreted, this increases one's level of anxiety and elicits more worries, inappropriate behaviors, and misdirected attention.

I use the term *internal distractor* to refer to sources of interference from within such as task-irrelevant thoughts and disturbing emotional arousal. During test-taking the most common and most interfering internal distractor is disruptive mental activity in the form of *worries, panicky thinking,* and *negative self-evaluations.* I introduced you to a few examples of this disruptive mental activity in Chapter 2. Recall that when Brian was in stressful academic situations, he beset himself with a host of worries and panicky inner speech:

> "What if I go totally blank tomorrow?"
> "Why can't I concentrate better?"
> "I'm already in a hole!"
> "You screwed up!"

Various specific categories of disruptive mental activity are detailed in Chapter 5. For now, the main point is that worries, panicky thinking, and self-evaluations are all examples of a *self*-oriented rather than a *task*-oriented attentional focus. Notice that Brian's thoughts center on self-concerns that preclude becoming absorbed in the task at hand. This self-oriented thinking (recall the earlier Sarason quote) results in the familiar negative yield: lowered test-taking efficiency and more anxiety.

Physiological and emotional distress constitute a second kind of internal distractor. Interestingly, extensive research indicates that physiological symptoms and anxious emotionality tend not to be as disruptive to academic performance as the self-oriented, worrisome thinking just described. Moreover, it is usually not the physiological and emotional distress, per se, that interferes with performance so much as it is the attention paid to this distress and the labeling of it as threatening and undesirable. Of course, if physiological distress and emotional arousal levels are very high, it becomes difficult to carry on with the task at hand.

Besides worry and emotionality, a third source of internal distraction has been identified[2], *task-generated interference*, which also occurs under stressful evaluative circumstances. Task-generated interference is formally defined as preoccupation with task-produced competing responses. Fortunately, the concept of task-generated interference is easier to grasp than its formal definition. Task-generated interference refers to the tendency for academically anxious students to get hung up on aspects of the test or evaluated task that are inefficient or relatively extraneous or both. Some examples:

thinking back during the test to previous questions,

persisting for an inappropriately long time with a question whose answer is not forthcoming,

thinking ahead to untried questions,

weighing in one's mind, again and again, the relative merits of two alternatives to a multiple-choice question,

[2] Deffenbacher, J.L. Worry, emotionality, and task-generated interference in test anxiety: An empirical test of attentional theory. *Journal of Educational Psychology*, 1978, 70, 248–254.

persisting with a particular approach for solving a question even though the approach is not yielding a satisfactory solution.

It is very important to become quickly aware when your attention has become too securely fixed on task-generated interference. I recommend sharpening your sense of self-awareness in this respect, since task-generated interference easily masquerades as task-focused, functional problem-solving. It is not. It only *seems* so and actually works counterproductively to stymie progress. Heightened self-awareness and effective utilization of coping responses are needed because task-generated interference is a powerful negative influence: incomplete answers and unsolved questions exert such a strong psychological pull that one is very tempted to return to or persist with them.

Reverie or *daydreaming* is a final example of an internal distraction. This distractor presents a problem most typically during studying. Coping Response #1 (stimulus control) can be used to reduce the interfering nature of daydreaming on studying. Other coping responses aimed at refocusing attention are suggested later in this chapter. Again, early awareness of this distractor and quick application of coping responses are the key: daydreams have a run-on quality that means it is easy to become totally absorbed in one and lose much valuable study time.

Psychologist Frank C. Richardson[3] has listed various self-oriented responses that aptly summarize some of the internal distractions onto which academically anxious students misdirect their attention:

[3] Richardson, F.C. A self study manual for students on coping with test-taking anxiety. *Technical Report No. 25*, Austin: University of Texas Computer Assisted Instruction Laboratory, 1973.

   i. worrying about your performance, including how
      well others are doing compared with you,
  ii. ruminating too long and fruitlessly over alter-
      native answers or responses,
 iii. being preoccupied with bodily reactions asso-
      ciated with anxiety,
  iv. ruminating about possible consequences of doing
      poorly on the test—disapproval, punishment,
      loss of status or esteem, damage to academic
      record or job chances,
   v. thoughts or feelings of inadequacy—this may
      include active self-criticism or self-condemnation,
      calling yourself "stupid," and so on.

We've looked at types of external and internal distractors, and now I'd like to mention one final attentional
problem affecting academically anxious students, *reduced
cue utilization*. Reduced cue utilization refers to the tendency of students under high levels of anxiety to distribute
their attention unevenly; what can happen is that the
range of task cues and the amount of information that
can be utilized become more and more restricted. For
example, students commonly remark: "I read the question
wrong. Where I read the word 'should', it really said
'should not'," Or: "I kept trying to solve the problem,
but the equations I used weren't working. Later I saw I
was omitting part of the given information that had been
included in the body of the question. Somehow I didn't
see it!"

These examples illustrate how relevant information or
cues that were embedded within the question did not get
attended to. Obviously, if valuable cues are not apprehended, it will have a negative effect on performance,
especially where fine discriminations must be made. An

understanding or appreciation of how reduced cue utilization poses difficulties can help suggest some special coping responses to counter this tendency. One such coping response is the adoption of calmer, smoother test-taking behaviors (covered in Chapter 6). Another is task-orienting self-directives, a particular kind of inner speech that can help marshal one's attentional capacity and keep one task-focused. Task-orienting self-directives as a coping response are discussed later in this chapter.

To summarize this section, we find that under stressful evaluative circumstances, academically anxious students tend to allow their attention to become deflected from the task at hand:

   i. attention may center on self-oriented concerns (such as worries or physiological arousal) rather than on task-focused problem-solving,
  ii. the external environment may be scanned, especially in order to seek clues regarding one's progress,
 iii. students may get hung up on less immediate or relatively extraneous aspects of the test or evaluation (task-generated interference),
 iv. relevant task cues or information embedded in test items may not be apprehended or attended to (reduced cue utilization).

Automation and Attentional Control?

"I don't know what to do to get my attention back on the task!" Such complaints are common from students who claim they can't concentrate. They wish for some kind of miracle or machine that could provide instant concentration. In our high-tech, computerized world, the development of such a device seems a tantalizing prospect—but one that is not without drawbacks.

It has long been known that the human brain emits several types of electrical activity that can be classified according to their frequency and amplitude as measured by an electroencephalograph. One type of brain-wave activity known as alpha typically occurs during moments of daydreaming or reverie, when eyes are closed, or when one stares blankly into space (lack of ocular fixation). A few years ago, Thomas Mulholland[4] suggested adopting EEG methods for detecting shifts in visual attention. Instruments that he called "attention controllers" could be used to monitor brain-wave activity and feed this information into a computer. If brain-wave responses were inappropriate (i.e., if alpha wave activity were detected), an alerting signal could be triggered to remind the student to stop daydreaming and resume attending to the task at hand. According to Mulholland, attention controllers might be incorporated, for example, into teaching machines.

Mulholland's suggestion has been realized by Professor Karel Montor[5] of the U.S. Naval Academy, who patented an "Attention-Level Analyzer." This EEG monitoring device is programmed to detect brain wave changes associated with shifts from mental concentration to aimless daydreaming, as when, for example, a student who is supposed to be working math problems lets attention drift off elsewhere. Once the analyzer detects the resulting

[4] Mulholland, T. Objective EEG methods for studying covert shifts of visual attention. In F.J. McGuigan & R.A. Schoonover (eds.), *The psychophysiology of thinking*, New York: Academic Press, 1973.

[5] Montor, K. Brain-wave research. *Naval Research Review*, 1973, 26, 7–11.

alpha activity, a tone sounds alerting the student to direct attention back to the task at hand.

However, there are a couple of drawbacks to this kind of attention-controlling device. One obvious limitation is that such equipment is available to only a few students. Second, detecting the presence of alpha activity doesn't automatically cure the problem of misfocused attention. Why not?

Another type of brain-wave activity, beta, has a higher frequency range and is associated with intense concentration on mental tasks. This wave pattern corresponds to mental attentiveness. When the attention-controlling machine picks up beta, it assumes that concentration and attentiveness are occurring, and hence no alerting signal would be sounded. However, beta activity is also elicited by worry, anxiety, and apprehension. Thus, if a student's attention were intensely directed onto self-oriented worries, physical symptoms of anxiety, or task-generated interference, the machine would be no wiser—all this mental work registers in the beta range, even though it is detrimental to performance. To the machine, all of this negative concentration looks like "good" beta.

Instruments like the Attention-Level Analyzer have much to offer. Yet we shall probably have to wait until a higher level of technical sophistication is achieved to bring us instrumentation that can discriminate between qualitatively different kinds of beta wave-producing mental activity and that can train individuals to increase their problem-solving capacity.[6]

If technology is not yet the answer, we shall have to look elsewhere for alternative coping solutions to the problem

---

[6] For more information regarding this concept of brain-wave biofeedback, the interested reader might consult: Brown, B. B., *Stress and the art of biofeedback*. New York: Harper & Row, 1973, pp. 151–152.

of misdirected attention. Coping responses suggested in the next section address three aspects of the problem: (a) simple redirection of attention back on task after distraction; (b) coping with reduced cue utilization; and (c) dealing with the breakdown of concentration following frustration.

Managing Misdirected Attention

Directing attention back on task. The key here is developing quick awareness of precisely when and where attention has been misdirected. Once you are aware that concentration has been broken or that thoughts have become irrelevant to the task at hand, such awareness can be used as an alerting signal to return attention back on target. This process of awareness of misdirected attention and subsequent redirection to the academic task is especially important during exams, when optimal task-focused attention is desired. In this chapter's introduction, I discussed the likelihood of attention being sidetracked during stressful academic evaluations and detailed some common sources of distraction. Now that you are familiar with the distractors, let's hone your awareness of them as they crop up during academic tasks. To accomplish this, I suggest you perform a "homework" exercise the next time you study. It takes only twenty to thirty minutes. Here's what to do:

i. Have a sheet of lined notebook paper next to you while you study.
ii. Make a special effort to monitor your attention and be aware each time it goes off track.
iii. Log and describe the distraction.
iv. After doing this for about twenty minutes, go back

to each entry and identify or label what type of distraction it was.

For example, a student performed this exercise while writing an outline for a short paper, and her first few entries looked like this:

Where Attention Got Misdirected	Type of Distraction
1. Noticed I was playing around with my ballpoint pen	1. External distractor: irrelevant behavior
2. Thinking about how much I hate this assignment	2. Internal distractor: self-oriented thought
3. Kept getting hung up over the wording of the introductory paragraph	3. Task-generated interference
4. Worried that I'll never get this done before deadline	4. Internal distractor: self-oriented thinking
5. Glancing over at roommate's newspaper	5. External distractor
6. Thinking about what I'll wear tomorrow	6. Internal distractor: daydreaming

You probably experienced many breaks of attention during this exercise. We can exploit your awareness of attentional lapses in order to maximize efficiency and minimize the negative effect of self-oriented mental activity. These comprise the goals of *Coping Response #3: Redirecting Attention to Task.* This deceptively simple coping response is one of the most frequently used; thus, becoming adept at employing it will definitely be to your advantage.

With Coping Response #3, often all that is required is acknowledging as soon as possible a lapse of attention or the presence of task-irrelevant thinking and then turning attention back on task. Sometimes giving yourself a simple self-reminder or self-directive (e.g., "There you go again, worrying about not finishing on time . . . eyes back onto the test paper . . . ") helps you refocus. However, as I said, this is a deceptively simple coping response because of the manner in which it is appropriately performed.

First, it is desirable to adopt a *passive* attitude when redirecting attention; by that I mean avoid becoming angry or disappointed with yourself because your attention strayed. All that is needed is to acknowledge that your attention has strayed and matter-of-factly, passively turn your attention back on task. Sometimes students expect themselves to be supremely attentive and believe that self-directed anger or sharp commands help motivate themselves to be attentive. Such emotional overreactions are unnecessary.

A second difficulty is that recognizing and correcting attentional lapses is an ongoing process that must be repeated numerous times. Again, some students expect that their attention should respond perfectly after only a few corrections. By not accepting the fact that attentional corrections must be made continually, they set themselves up to experience certain frustration. Then they abandon this coping response with the remark: "It doesn't work!" For those readers who have had practice with some meditative or relaxation techniques, there is an obvious parallel with Coping Response #3. You may have been instructed to focus attention on a stimulus such as a sound, word, or breathing cadence, and each time your attention strayed to an extraneous thought you were to passively return to the stimulus.[7] During a 15- to 20-minute relaxation

[7] See, for example, Benson, H. *The relaxation response.* New York: William Morrow, 1975.

period you may have needed to correct yourself many times.

I recommend that you first practice Coping Response #3 a few times while studying or doing homework. Once you have achieved some proficiency with redirecting attention in studying situations, apply this coping response during quizzes and exams. To summarize, Coping Response #3 consists of the following steps:

   i. Note any drift of attention to distractions or task-irrelevant thinking.
  ii. Acknowledge this lapse of attention and redirect attention back to task at hand.
 iii. Adopt a passive, matter-of-fact attitude when redirecting; no need to get frustrated with oneself for not having unwavering attention.
  v. Repeat this procedure as needed; redirecting attention is an ongoing process.

Coping with reduced cue utilization. As was mentioned earlier, reduced cue utilization refers to the tendency of academically anxious students to fail to apprehend facts or information. To deal with this anxiety handicap, the coping response suggested in this section involves learning how to "talk" to oneself in such a way as to guide one through an academic task. Using inner speech may sound novel or strange to you, but it is actually a powerful behavioral control tool that we all use in numerous situations each day. Let's first examine how we can generate this kind of "internal dialogue" to deal with the problem of reduced cue utilization:

As far as statistical problems are concerned, Chris has the math skills to solve them, but she makes careless mistakes on tests and homework sets that bring down her grade. She may not attend to information that is embedded in the problem, or she may become momentarily flustered, try to hurry herself, and then leave out an important step. She decided she needed to minimize this tendency, so on a recent homework exercise she experimented with using internal speech in such a way as to guide herself through the solution of each problem. This internal dialogue of self-instructions helped her keep track of each step in the problem-solving process and acted as a kind of personal system of checks and balances to keep herself oriented and attentive. If we could listen in on her internal dialogue as she solved the first problem, excerpts from it would sound like this: "Okay. Read the question slowly . . . What are they asking for in this question? They want me to calculate the standard deviation for these 20 scores . . . Now first write down the given information . . . Okay, go back through the chapter and find the right equation to use . . . Write it down and plug the given information into it . . . Let's see, I've got to calculate the deviation of each score from the mean and square the result . . . For the first score that's 17 minus 14, squaring it yields 9 . . . Now sum up all the squared deviations . . . Remember, they're asking for the standard deviation, so you've got to take the square roiot of the variance . . . "

Notice how Chris utilizes various self-commands and self-instructions in order to talk herself through the problem step by step. With this approach she is less likely to miss information or make a miscalculation. Chris' example illustrates the use of *Coping Response #4, Task-Orienting Self-Directives (TOSD's)*. Like Coping Response #3 (Redirecting Attention), Task-Orienting Self-Directives are a basic, frequently employed coping response that is important for you to master.

Let's examine some of the rationale behind TOSD's. Throughout the day, each of us engages in a steady stream of self-conversation that can take many forms. We talk to ourselves about incidents from the past or imagine future situations. We perform self-dialogues whereby problems are solved or decisions are made. We make evaluative statements about our behavior. We use inner speech to praise or condemn our efforts. We use other inner speech in the form of self-instructions to guide ourselves through to the completion of a task. Much of this self-talk is performed with only minimal awareness. For example, as I learned to parallel park a car, I had to deliberately talk my way through the procedure using stepwise self-instructions; now that I've mastered the skill, I'm only minimally aware of the brief mental notation needed to maneuver the car into its spot.

Task-Orienting Self-Directives are specific self-instructions designed to keep behavior on target, to offer problem-solving approaches, to assist in guiding ourselves through to problem resolution, and to keep attention task-focused. What I'm suggesting is that you make wholly *deliberate* and *conscious* the kind of self-instructional inner speech in which you subliminally engage throughout the day. We want to exploit and capitalize on the power of inner speech to assist in keeping attention and behavior task-directed.

As I write I'm reminded (of all things!) of my golf game. Actually, I talk myself through a series of TOSD's each time I address the ball ("Get the ball opposite left heel," "take club away from the ball slowly," "square feet, hips, and shoulders on line with the target"). These directives help me be aware of and correct for subtle but important flaws that could otherwise cause my swing to come apart.

We began this discussion of TOSD's for combating the problem of reduced cue utilization. Let's return to Chris' example to see how she used TOSD's to help herself become more aware of available cues and information and to reduce careless mistakes. Her example suggests several points for employing TOSD's to your own advantage.

1. Self-instructions for controlling *pacing* are important. Note Chris' TOSD: "Read the question slowly." Academically anxious students miss cues by working too speedily.

2. Explicitly stating the problem to be solved is especially valuable for orienting one's attention and efforts. Return to Chris' example and see how she engages in this type of internal dialogue.

3. If you are performing quantitative work, talk yourself through arithmetic or mathematical computations in order to reduce chances of error.

4. Use simple self-commands to guide behavior (e.g., "Write down the given information"; "Sum up the squared deviations"). Again, the aim of TOSD's is to make as deliberate and conscious as possible the steps and procedures usually taken for granted.

5. Practice talking yourself through the step-by-step procedures needed to solve a problem. Note Chris' example here. Remember, academically anxious students tend to let their attention wander onto task-irrelevant thinking, and one way to resist this tendency is to intentionally engage in this kind of task-specific self-talk.

6. Freely use self-reminders to help keep procedures in mind and reduce errors. Recall how Chris

reminded herself to take the square root for her calculations.

One word of emphasis: too often, academically anxious students fail to appreciate that they truly operate under attentional and behavioral handicaps and that they need to take advantage of every angle in order to minimize those handicaps. Instead, some students shortcut these suggestions when they really should be practiced and implemented conscientiously and without modification.

Dealing with the breakdown of concentration following frustration. A third troublesome situation occurs when academically anxious students encounter a setback of frustration while working. Frequently, two kinds of inappropriate reactions follow from frustration. First, task-focused concentration is broken as the student engages in self-oriented thinking and anxiety-engendering self-talk, including expressions of futility and worries. Second, when frustration blocks progress, the student can be momentarily stuck on how to proceed; during these nonproductive dry spells, it is easy to become less engrossed in the task, thereby increasing susceptibility to distraction. To counter these inappropriate reactions, we turn again to our use of self-instructions and task-orienting self-directives. This time we wish to cultivate an internal dialogue in which you suggest to yourself alternative, creative, and flexible strategies for dealing with a blocked path or setback. Let me emphasize the importance of applying these TOSD's immediately upon awareness of the early signs of frustration—before your feelings of helplessness get too far out of hand. A couple of examples illustrate the use of TOSD's in this kind of circumstance:

> Rob habitually met with much frustration when writing papers. He agonized over the choice of words,

got angry with himself if sentences failed to convey his intended meaning, and experienced long dry spells where nothing would be put on paper. To correct this situation, it was suggested that he develop self-directives to serve as cues for getting his attention back on task and away from distractions. It was further suggested that his internal dialogue contain some directives for inducing elements of creativity and flexibility into his work—commodities that would help absorb himself into the task and thus reduce susceptibility to distraction. This new approach built upon Rob's sense of self-awareness. Immediately upon awareness of any snag in progress, expression of futility, or attention lapse, Rob engaged in a combination of self-reminders and self-directives to guide himself through his work, in this case a short paper for a psychology course:

Problems		TOSD's
Frustrating self by thinking that sentences do not hang together properly	⟶ Awareness ⟶	"Just let the ideas and words flow . . . Even if they do sound a bit disjointed or stilted"
Staring at blank page; growing sense of frustration with slow progress	⟶ Awareness ⟶	"Remember, this is just a first draft . . . You're allowed to make a few mistakes . . . All you want for now are the raw ideas"
Frustrating self with belief that writing should be at a certain level of sophistication	⟶ Awareness ⟶	"Say it in your own words . . . You don't have to force yourself to make it sound 'psychological'"

Expressing futility at ——→ Awareness ——→ "There you go again,
never being able to   getting stuck on
choose most appropriate   the 'right' word to
word   use . . . Just leave a
                                                                    blank space and go back
                                                                    to it later . . . You can
                                                                    live with that bit of
                                                                    ambiguity"

Ruth utilized self-directives during a test situation. She was taking a math exam and was stumped on a question. Ordinarily this would be an occasion for severe distraction—frantic and panicky thinking, scanning the testing room, focusing on physical feelings of anxiety. However, this time after she became aware of the early signs of panic, she chose instead several appropriate TOSD's that would reorient her to the task and prime her for a creative approach to the predicament.

Problems   *TOSD's*

Feeling urge to push ——→ Awareness ——→ "Whoa . . . Take it
self faster in order to get   easy . . . No need to
through exam   unravel . . . Give
                                                                    yourself a moment to let
                                                                    some ideas percolate"

Scanning classroom to ——→ Awareness ——→ "You won't get much
see how other students   help looking around . . .
are handling exam   Eyes back onto paper"

Frustrated by her ——→ Awareness ——→ "Remember, he covered
momentary inability to   this in class . . . Just
recall information   let your mind go back to
                                                                    the notes you took that
                                                                    day . . . see in your
                                                                    mind's eye how your
                                                                    notes from that lecture
                                                                    appeared on the page"

Experiences setback of ⟶ Awareness ⟶ "Look at the problem
being unable to obtain again, but this time play
reasonable answer to around with the
question numbers . . . Take a new
approach . . . Try
plugging in some new
variables . . . Go ahead
and first do a few sample
calculations on scratch
paper."

Knowing how to cope with frustration is an integral part of managing the emotional side of academics. Frequently I encounter students who, after experiencing a setback, lose their task-focused train of thought. TOSD's, if applied appropriately, can benefit you in several ways. First, you can use them as signals to anchor your attention on task. Second, you can instruct yourself to generate alternative methods for coping with "stuckness"—which is what frustration is all about. Note how Ruth used self-directives to attack the exam question from a different perspective. Finally, self-directives can induce in you a creative, flexible mind-set that is important for helping you become absorbed in your work. Interestingly, it has been shown experimentally that these kinds of short, relatively simple self-directives can engender creative thinking in college students.[8]

In order to develop TOSD's to cope with misdirected attention during frustrating situations, I've outlined the suggestions below:

[8] Meichenbaum, D. Enhancing creativity by modifying what subjects say to themselves. *American Educational Research Journal*, 1975, *12*, 129–145.

Tips for Applying TOSD's

1. Frustration is likely to occur in test or academic situations where efforts are not meeting with success, where progress is stymied, or correct answers to questions are not forthcoming.
2. Be alert as to where attention can be diverted during these circumstances:
   a. onto feelings of anxious arousal
   b. onto expressions of futility or self-criticism
   c. onto worries
   d. onto external distractors (clock, other students, etc.).
3. Watch for behavior reactions to frustration:
   a. getting hung up on task-irrelevant behavior
   b. long pauses where no work is being accomplished.

To Formulate the Content of TOSD's

1. Check back over the Rob and Ruth examples and use their self-directives as models for your own.

2. But *use your own words*. Don't parrot these examples. Develop a set of self-directives that you will *really* listen to. After all, TOSD's do no good if you don't follow the directive.

3. Phrase your self-directives in such a way that they:
   a. *"pull" for creativity and flexibility* for overcoming the frustrating situation ("Just let the ideas and words flow"; You're allowed to make a few mistakes")
   b. *help you to size up the task.* ("Look at the problem again"; "Try plugging in some new variables")
   c. *suggest an appropriate work pace* ("Whoa . . . take it easy"; "Give yourself a moment to let some ideas percolate")
   d. *remind you to direct attention* on task ("Eyes back onto your paper"; "Just let your mind go back to the notes you took that day").

4. Immediately upon awareness of these signs of frustration, perform directives to help get attention task-focused and to facilitate absorption into task.
5. Get some practice using your own TOSD's. You might practice self-directives, for example, while:
   a. doing computational problems
   b. writing or debugging a computer program
   c. translating passages into a foreign language
   d. writing a term paper.

Summary

Misdirected attention is one of the primary problems facing academically anxious students. In this chapter we have outlined some of the sources of distraction and problems attendant to misdirected attention. Coping Response #3, Redirecting Attention, was introduced as a useful procedure in exam situations. The problems of reduced cue utilization and misdirected attention following frustration were also discussed. I suggested that marshaling one's powers of inner speech could prove useful in managing these two problems. Task-Orienting Self-Directives (TOSD's) as Coping Response #4 were described whereby a student can self-instruct for task-focused attention. It was mentioned that coping Response #4 would assist a student to absorb himself or herself in a task and hence improve concentration.

CHAPTER 5

Brands of Disruptive Self-Talk and Mental Activity

Introduction

I shall begin this chapter by asking you to perform a little exercise:

For the next minute or two, imagine a recent test situation, one in which you experienced some emotional difficulty. Try, in your mind's eye, to imagine yourself back in the exam room. Picture where you were seated. Recall the configuration of the room, seating arrangements, other students. Really go back into that time and place. Now try to recall your thoughts before and during the exam. What do you remember thinking about or saying to yourself? If it helps, close your eyes to better reperceive both the "video" and "audio" portions of that event . . .

Now, while your thoughts are still fresh in mind, take pen and paper and *write down* as precisely as you can the *specific* (word-for-word) thoughts, self-talk, self-instructions, or other mental activity you could recall. Save these sentences for an upcoming exercise. How did this exercise go for you? If your experience was similar to that of my academically anxious clients, you probably conjured up a batch of unpleasant or embarrassing thoughts and images that reflected the disastrousness of the situation.

This exercise teases out some of the toxic, anxiety-engendering mental activity that occurs during stressful exams and academic evaluations. In Chapter 4 we discussed how we all engage in frequent self-dialogue, and we strove to harness some of the positive power of internal speech by designing task-orienting self-directives to facilitate task-focused attention. Counselors and psychologists have observed that during stressful evaluative situations academically anxious students emit a distinctive mixture of thoughts and self-talk that tends to have a deleterious effect on performance. Instead of emitting positive, planful thinking when confronted with stressful circumstances, students may engage in varieties of disruptive mental activity that *feed back into the anxiety and interfere with effective problem-solving.*

In the next section various categories of disruptive and interfering mental activity are presented, with excerpts borrowed from actual counseling sessions. The purpose is to help you develop a greater awareness of these kinds of poisonous thoughts so that coping responses can be subsequently initiated. In the last section I detail some alternative, adaptive cognitive modes to substitute for the anxiety-engendering kind. But before we begin these discussions, I will close this section by examining types of stressful evaluative situations that trigger disruptive mental activity.

Of course, any number of situations are likely to be interpreted as stressful, but Irwin Sarason[1] has suggested three general categories, to which I would like to add a fourth:

1. *Well-defined* (i.e., *unambiguous*) *situations commonly seen as threatening and to which the student believes he or she cannot respond adequately.* Giving a speech before a large class, for example, is a clear-cut task and one commonly interpreted as threatening: an adequate or satisfactory performance is not guaranteed—the audience may be bored, the speaker may become forgetful, and so forth.

   Academic situations also take on a threatening quality if the student believes he or she is incapable of handling them. In psychological terms we say such an unconfident individual is low in *perceived self-efficacy* ("efficacy" meaning effectiveness). Math is an academic area in which low self-efficacy often surfaces. Perhaps a student who otherwise would be reasonably proficient at math had some unfortunate experiences with it, from which a generalization is made that he or she is "lousy" at all math. Consequently, the student avoids all tasks involving math, and on those occa-

[1] Sarason, I.G. The test anxiety scale: Concept and research. In C.D. Spielberger and I.G. Sarason (eds.), *Stress and Anxiety* (Vol. 5), Washington, D.C.: Hemishpere Publishing, 1978.

sions when confrontation with math is unavoidable the student expresses a lack of self-efficacy ("I can't do it"), rehearses for failure, and emits a stream of task-disruptive inner speech.

Of course, one of the surest ways to feel incapable of responding to an academic task is to be unprepared for it. Thus, adequate preparation and review are essential for a self-assured approach to exams.

2. *Ambiguous situations in which the student must structure task requirements and personal expectations.* As academic situations become less and less structured, students tend to feel more and more uncomfortable. This uncomfortableness is reflected in the inner speech of students who are experiencing an intolerable degree of situational ambiguity: "How do they expect you to do this?"; "I'll never figure this out!"; "What's the use?" Remember, too, that academically anxious students scan their environment looking for clues as to how they are progressing or what they should be doing. When the situation is ambiguous, few such clues are available, and this poses a problem as to how one should cope.

Consider an English teacher who gives her class nothing more than the vague assignment: "Write a theme." Many students find those instructions unacceptable and assertively request more structure. A few students, feeling uncomfortable with the ambiguity, set themselves to work and "do their own thing." Others cope less well, perhaps telling themselves that the situation is impossible or copying what someone else does.

Those familiar with standardized college admission tests (e.g., SAT, ACT) may recall being provided with extensive pretest instructions and sample questions. Such preparatory materials reduce situational ambiguity and better insure a more adaptive approach to the test.

3. *Situations defined in idiosyncratic ways.* Sometimes students are confronted by situations which, because of personal experience or prior learning, present a uniquely personal threat. For a particular student certain types of skills, evaluation methods, or interpersonal situations may be imbued with much negative psychological significance. For example, some students encounter no debilitating anxiety unless faced with situations involving dreaded math problems; perhaps due to prior traumatic experiences with math or a perceived lack of math ability, these students come to regard math stimuli as negative events. Similar negative interpretations might follow from situations requiring various verbal skills or mechanical aptitudes. Different types of evaluation methods (multiple-choice or essay questions or oral presentations) may elicit untoward reactions depending on one's idiosyncratic "makeup." Sometimes students find certain interpersonal situations emotionally trying, as when conferring with an august faculty advisor.

4. *Situations in which a setback or reversal frustrates progress.* I include this is a special fourth category to Sarason's three general stressful evaluative situations. Frequently, I find that when a student's progress on a task is blocked due to a mistake, lack of knowledge, or other setback this situation

becomes an occasion for calamitous and task-interfering inner speech. Many students, upon experiencing a setback, almost automatically interpret it as a catastrophic event, thereby eliciting an anxiety reaction. In order to control academic anxiety, it is important to be aware of exactly what you tell yourself after a setback.

When academically anxious students are thrust into these general stressful situations, there occurs a kind of "systems malfunction." Attention is sidetracked. Task-appropriate behavior unravels. Physiological indicators of anxiety make their presence felt. And above all, a blend of internal speech is emitted that both reflects and exacerbates one's state of uncertainty and interferes with effective problem resolution. I must emphasize, of course, that the situation itself is not so much responsible for anxiety as is what students tell themselves about the situation. This point should become clear as we detail in the next section the categories and content of the inner speech of academically anxious students.

Brands of Disruptive Self-Talk and Mental Activity

What follows is a detailed look at the fear-producing mental activity that is characteristic of the academically anxious student. I think you'll see that it is a smorgasbord of self-talk and personalized thinking that literally guarantees anxiety and ineffective coping. We think of the stereotypical anxious student as paralyzed by emotionality and physiological manifestations of anxiety. But surprisingly, the bulk of research indicates that disruptive thought processes have a more negative impact on academic performance. For example, Morris and Liebert[2], in a sample of college students, found that "worry" (e.g., believing others are brighter, concern about possible failure) had a significantly more adverse effect on performance than did emotionality.

Again the plan for this chapter is to help you, through examples, to begin to identify this kind of mental activity in yourself and then to apply alternative thinking and inner speech that are incompatible with and can substitute for this fear-producing and task-disruptive kind.

1. The first category I term *panicky self-talk*. Since many panicky self-talk sentences begin with the words, "Oh, God," I sometimes facetiously refer to this category as "Oh, Godisms." Panicky self-talk is characterized by frantic verbalizations and a sense of diminishing self-control over the academic situation. Take a look at the following examples from students recalling their thoughts during a test or an academic task:

   "There isn't enough time! There's still so much I don't know!"

   An older, returning student describes his reaction after scanning the other students in his drawing class: "I looked around at the sketches everyone was doing and said to myself: 'My God, I didn't expect such good work from mere kids!'"

[2] Morris, L.W., and Liebert, R.M. Relationship of cognitive and emotional components of test anxiety to physiological arousal and academic performance. *Journal of Consulting and Clinical Psychology*, 1970, 35, 332–337.

"What's this notation he's using? Where did he get that from? What's going on?"

"Oh, God . . . maybe this will turn out to be too hard!"

"So there I stood in front of the class, and I told myself: 'You're losing everyone's interest.'"

"I'm so lost on the first day of class, imagine what the rest of the semester will be like."

Student sees classmates turning in test papers early and interjects: "Good Lord, how can they be done so soon?"

"Oh, God, now I'm starting to get nervous!"

"I stared at the first question and thought: 'What is this? I don't understand it. It looks like some foreign language.' At that moment I knew that I was really in trouble."

"This test is so long! Here I've busted my hump for 45 minutes and there's still so much to do!"

I think you can begin to appreciate that panicky self-talk, as well as the other varieties of anxiety-engendering mental activity we shall encounter, works to further handicap the student in already difficult academic situations by:

   i. Shifting attention away from the task to self-oriented concerns;

  ii. increasing panic and one's senses of vulnerability and uncertainty;

 iii. reducing one's feeling of self-assuredness;

 iv. portraying the situation in overly serious, dramatic tones—a kind of negative hyperbolic effect;

    v. failing to suggest useful coping approaches to the problem situation.

Watch for these handicaps as we cover the remaining categories.

    2. *"Why" questions and "If only" statements* comprise the second category.

       "Why" questions seem reasonable enough . . .

       "Why can't I concentrate?"

       "Why do they make us memorize this stuff?"

       "Why does it always take me longer to do this than anybody else?"

       "Why don't these concepts stick in my head? Why isn't it clear?"

       "Why did I ever decide to go pre-med?"

. . . yet they are fundamentally unanswerable. In fact, one question usually begets others: Why, indeed, can't I concentrate? I dunno, maybe because I'm not motivated. Why aren't I motivated? Maybe because I haven't learned to discipline myself. Why haven't . . . and on and on. These questions are usually quite complex and yield no easy answers. More often than not, "why" questions are as much a waste of time as wishful thinking such as:

       "If only I had 20 more I.Q. points."

       "If only I had gone to a better high school."

The problem with "Why" questions and "If only" statements is that they tend to reinforce feelings of helplessness, frustration, and anger. Be alert for their presence in your own inner speech.

3. Category number three is a form of worrisome thinking based on a *"What if . . . ?"* sentence construction. You've already been introduced to this troublemaker in Chapters 2 and 3. "What if . . . ?" thinking is especially dangerous because you can fill in the blank with the disaster of your choice: What if . . .

> . . . I turn in a paper and it doesn't have enough references?

> . . . my final exam grade turns out as bad as my grades on the midterms?

> . . . my best isn't good enough?

> . . . I can't get the review done on time?

> . . . I get the points confused?

> . . . my business school application is turned down?

> . . . I am handed the exam and "block"?

> . . . my roommate "aces" the exam and I louse up? I've lost too much face already.

> . . . it turns out that I've actually gotten through school all these years on trickery? Maybe I don't have any skill at all!

Some worries are disguised in other sentence structures, but they can easily be translated into a "What if . . . ?" construction:

> "Maybe this will prove too hard for me."

Read as: "What if this proves too hard for me?"

"There are times when I doubt I can learn all there is to learn and become a practicing lawyer."

Read as: "What if I can't learn all there is to learn and never become a lawyer?"

"I could know the material cold, but the grading could be arbitrary."

Read as: "What if I know the material cold but am penalized by arbitrary grading?"

A defining characteristic of anxiety is the fear and apprehension of uncertainty. Not only does "What if . . . ?" thinking set oneself up to be inordinately sensitized to and fearful of the unknown, but it also implies an inability to cope with unfavorable contingencies.

4. One of the biggest problem areas for many students is *negative and critical self-statements.* This brand of self-talk can be extremely insidious.

DOONESBURY   by Garry Trudeau

How many kinds of anxiety-producing mental activity can you find here?

When faced with academic challenge, some students seem to automatically activate in their minds a tape recorder filled with self-expletives. You can subject yourself to a vicious torrent of verbal self-abuse without being aware of its effect on your performance and sense of self-confidence. Check out these examples:

Student putting into words her experience when asked to do demonstration before class: "I felt so inexperienced. I said to myself, 'I'm stupid, inept; I don't know what I'm doing here.'"

Military veteran entering school as freshman architecture student: "I'm twenty-four and I don't have one damn creative idea in my head . . . My goal this first semester is to know I'm not as bad as I think."

"No one respects me, least of all my so-called best friends."

"I feel so dumb because I don't grasp this material with ease."

"Like with my last test, it was so hard it was a joke, and it got to the point where I didn't even care. Just write anything down. Just get it over with. That's how I know I'm a quitter."

"You can bet that if I'm feeling like I have a good chance to do well, I'll really screw up."

"I shouldn't be so slow; I shouldn't be so sloppy. I'm so clumsy, too, that I attract attention to myself."

Of course, virtually all of this is unrealistically pessimistic and works to reinforce students' feelings of hopelessness. Moreover, negative and critical self-statements abound in the internal dialogue of students who claim that they aren't their old, self-confident selves. It's little surprise they feel so weak, since this kind of self-talk would undermine anyone's self-confidence.

5. Category number five, *unfavorable comparison to others*, is closely related to number four. With almost knee-jerk reliability many academically anxious students rate everyone else as superior in intelligence, academic savvy, "self-discipline," or other characteristics. Typical in this regard are the following student comments:

> Vet student involved with several classmates in giving injections to dogs: "Everyone else has had experience with injections . . . I even needed help filling the needle . . . compared to everyone else I felt inferior."

> "They say in our design class you're supposed to learn from other students, but when I see what everybody else is doing, I feel bad because I couldn't come up with those ideas myself."

> "The fellow I study with knows everything. Next to him I know nothing."

> "I feel more nervous when I watch the clock. Other people can use time to motivate themselves, but it only makes me more tense."

> "I'll tell myself: you can't compete with those smart cookies."

If you could tune in to the thought process of academically anxious students, you might hear the following sentences strung together: "Nobody in this course has as much trouble as I do! I'm hopeless! and I'm only getting worse! Why can't I get a better grip on myself?" This burst of negativism can be written in equation form:

$$\begin{array}{c}\text{unfavorable}\\ \text{comparison}\\ \text{to others}\end{array} + \begin{array}{c}\text{negative}\\ \text{self-}\\ \text{statement}\end{array} + \begin{array}{c}\text{panicky}\\ \text{self-talk}\end{array} + \begin{array}{c}\text{"Why"}\\ \text{question}\end{array} = \begin{array}{c}\text{increased}\\ \text{anxiety}\end{array} + \begin{array}{c}\text{feelings}\\ \text{of}\\ \text{hopeless-}\\ \text{ness}\end{array}$$

Of course, some students choose an opposite approach and seek out others to whom they can compare themselves *favorably*. This "I'm wonderful compared to so-and-so" attitude imparts a bogus sense of grandiosity and is as inappropriate as comparisons of the unfavorable kind. Probably the best approach is to avoid comparison altogether and to rely on one's own judgment for assessing the relative effectiveness of performance. Thus, instead of stacking my behavior up against that of others, I would rather consider how I might improve myself in the future and determine whether I had turned in a *personally* responsible or satisfying effort.

6. Although not the kind of mental activity that necessarily fosters anxiety, category number six, *anger-engendering self-talk*, can be a formidable barrier to effective performance. Like anxiety, anger is an immobilizing emotion. It is not a contradiction to uncover a great deal of anger-engendering self-talk in academically anxious students. When anger isn't directed at them-

selves (as through negative and critical self-statement), it is directed toward courses, fellow students, professors, and the "system." Some examples:

"Chemistry sucks!"

"I hate that smug look on their faces . . . you know, the ones who are the teacher's pets."

"So I spend all night studying, and I still mess up on the test. Then kids who don't put in any effort at all get the high grades. That isn't fair!"

"If only my grade-grubbing classmates would be less competitive, my problems would be over."

"I hate it when all of your grade depends on just a couple of lousy exams!"

"Professor _____ is a jerk!"

"I turn my papers in on time but half the class manages to wheedle extensions out of the instructor. Can you blame me for being teed off?"

The bottom line of anger is that when we rail against people and events, we are insisting that somehow they should act differently: chemistry should be less aversive, fellow students shouldn't look so smug, others should put in a fair share of effort. But what are the chances of the world's conforming to fit one's wishes? Anger really represents a failure to cope. For example, angry self-talk affords no positive suggestions for managing the situation such as what one could do to make chemistry more enjoyable, or what would be an appropriately assertive approach for suggesting to the instructor more uniform grading policies. Also, anger implies that the reasons for our frustration and indignation lie outside of ourselves—it's somebody else's fault. Finally, since anger involves putting others down, it leaves the angry one with the rather dubious reward of self-rightousness.

7. The *evocation of frightening mental images* represents the seventh category. We have all experienced how envisioning a scary image or mental picture can result in twinges of panic. After I saw Alfred Hitchcock's *Psycho*, I was practically panic-stricken each time I showered, because I imagined that a mad slasher might be lurking behind my shower curtain. Often students use mental pictures rather than wordy self-dialogue to communicate to themselves. Sometimes one need only envision a few fragments to an entire scene in order to experience a substantial effect. You may recall from our case example of Brian in Chapter 2 that just a fleeting mental picture of his being returned a heavily corrected exam paper was sufficient to evoke powerful feelings of hopelessness and vulnerability. This an example of an *anticipatory* image.

Of course, we can also conjure up memories of regetted past events, as many academically anxious students do when they remember how worked up they became during a previous exam. (Frequently an anticipatory image will follow, as students see history repeating itself on the next exam.)

Since these dramatic mental images can produce quite an anxious response, be alert to their occurrence as in these examples:

Comments of architecture student regarding efforts to perfect his drawing technique: "I tried to view the mistakes I was making in a positive way, and I wanted to keep practicing and perfecting my technique. But all I saw was me making the same kind of dumb mistakes 'way down the road."

"To my amazement, there I sat staring at my math test, stumped for how to proceed, and what am I thinking about but some previous tests I choked on!"

"I could just see myself trying to explain to my father how I messed up this semester so badly!"

"Then when I think about the next day's exam—walking into the classroom, seeing the test in front of me—I start to feel real weak."

"I guess you could say that at the times I feel most discouraged about my studies I let these scenes from the past come over me—like when I quit the soccer team—and I feel worse, like I'll never let myself stick with anything long enough to accomplish something."

8. When faced with stressful circumstances, academically anxious students too often respond with *whining* and *expressions of futility*. "It's too hard," "I'm too tired," "I can't stand it," are some

typical whining themes. Students bemoan how futile or hopeless their situations seem: "How can I ever get all of this work done?"; "I won't be able to remember any of this stuff!"; "I'll flunk! I know I will!"

Other examples of this category include:

"As I was reviewing my notes in my mind, I just kept thinking: 'I don't care if I do well, I just want to get over this tension.'"

Example of "Why" question followed by expression of futility: "Toward the end of the exam everyone was leaving and I wondered: 'Why can't I finish on time?' I felt like I didn't know anything."

"At one point during the exam when I started getting nervous, I thought about making an effort to calm myself down, but then I figured, it doesn't matter, I'll just freeze anyway."

"I'll get to the [exam room] door and I'll wonder if I can pass . . . I'll wish I could leave . . . I'm resigned to failure."

"While studying I start to bite my fingernails, fidget, get up, go to the kitchen. I feel less and less settled. After a point, I'll feel fatigued, even though I haven't done anything. It's fruitless to go on."

Notice the content of these self-talk excerpts. Each expresses some lack of self-efficacy or lack of perceived stamina or expectations of failure. The mental set suggested by this internal dialogue can result in a half-hearted or haphazard attempt to cope with the stressful situation, almost insuring failure. This is the classic *self-fulfilling prophecy*: failure is predicted; efforts to stave off failure are subintentionally ineffective; and failure, as predicted, occurs.

9. *Erroneous "If . . . then" conclusions*. We all are in a continuous process of trying to discover what is true for ourselves, of developing a personal system for understanding how the world operates and how we might effectively behave in the world. As part of this process, we are taught various rules of conduct, and we generate other rules as a result of our contact with the world. Furthermore, as we collect data from personal experience, our powers of reasoning allow us to draw conclusions and assumptions that help bring order to the vast array of situations confronting us daily. There are certain rules of thumb and sensible conclusions that many students would subscribe to and try to abide by. For example:

> If you can't get a particular multiple-choice question, then go on to the next one.

> If you've got an important exam tomorrow, then an adequate amount of sleep the night before is essential.

However, some of the conclusions we use to guide our behavior are of questionable validity, and others are downright fallacious. Sometimes we give ourselves rules that actually work to our detriment in the sense that thereby we may put extra pressure on ourselves, be less inclined to take risks, and limit our range of choices. For instance, one workaholic student told me (and presumably tells himself): "If I ease up on myself, then I'll come to love free time so much that I'll never go back to doing any work. Believe me, if you give me a little free time, I go out of control!" Let's look at the implications underlying the conclusions this student has drawn that mediate his behavior:

   i. It is obvious that he exerts undue pressure on himself ("I can't ease up").

   ii. His range of personal freedom is restricted since he forbids himself work breaks.

   iii. Is the assumption warranted that he *really* cannot go back to work after a respite? Or has he convinced himself of a spurious lack of self-control? Perhaps he has a track record of mismanaging free time, but does that mean he is destined to repeat those mistakes? Are past and future behaviors causally linked?

Watch out! These personal rules and assumptions *seem* to make sense. It is so easy to let this kind of thinking slip by, to swallow it unquestioningly, and to let it govern behavior when it should be vigorously confronted and checked out. What observations do you make about academic life and your academic life-style? Are the conclusions or assumptions warranted? Is there proof to back them up? Take a critical look at the student quotes below. Are they valid, invalid, or is there insufficient information to tell?

"If I screw up a test, then my self-esteem is shattered."

"If I don't like a subject, I can't get interested in it."

"If I make a mistake or waste time, then I should come down hard on myself because that's how you prevent future mistakes."

"If I worry about my schoolwork, I won't be caught unprepared."

"If I don't understand something right off, I'm a cinch to panic."

"If I miss a deadline for a paper, I don't deserve a second chance."

Statement of science major who was preventing herself from getting involved in the science courses: "If I follow a scientific path, the aesthetic parts of me will be extinguished."

"If I can just get to the test without getting upset, I'll be all right."

"If people saw my low grades, I couldn't live it down."

"If I'm able to get the first few problems on a test, I start to feel more confident."

"If I don't have absolute peace and quiet while I study, I can't get anything done."

"If you always try to do your best, people won't get a bad impression of you."

10. *Absolutistic thinking.* Take a look at the student quotes below. What might they all have in common?

    i. "I can't accept myself at times if I do less than what I expect of myself. I've got to be perfect."

    ii. Comment of community college transfer student trying to adjust to vigorous university demands: "I have to prove myself to other students . . . I ought to know what's going on."

    iii. "To prove to myself that I'm good at a subject, I must know it cold. But I get frustrated having to master the material."

    iv. "I need to get at least a 2.70 G.P.A."

    v. "If I take some time off or indulge myself, there's this voice inside telling me: 'You should be studying.'"

    vi. "I shouldn't be so slow . . . It shouldn't take me so much time!"

    vii. "My father has supported my schooling all these years, and I must not let him down."

    viii. "I'll get to the door [of the exam room] and I'll think: 'I can't afford to screw it up. I've got to pass. There's no two ways about it.'"

The clue is in the choice of verbs. "Got to's," "must's, "should's," ought's," "can't's," and "have to's" abound. These quotes are examples of *absolutistic thinking.* Students who operate out of absolutistic frameworks are demanding that their performance, personal attributes, and situations must be of a certain quality or yield certain results. Absolutistic thinking lies near the core of the problem of academic anxiety. Psychologists have long recognized the role that absolutistic thinking plays in anxiety and have coined such terms as "tyranny of the should"[3] and "*mus*turbation"[4] to point out its negative effect.

Absolutistic self-dialogues are usually the verbalizations that result from the four implicit special meanings students impose on academics (see Chapter 3). Thus, performance must be up to par lest: future plans be catastrophically spoiled (see quote viii); significant others be let down (see quote vii); one feel less worthy as a person (see quote i); or one lose the respect of others (see quote ii).

This demandingness places students under at least three crippling handicaps. Quote vi illustrates one such handicap. If a person's work capacity tops out at a given rate, it is unrealistic to assume that he or she can work any faster. Demanding more than one can produce leads to self-*un*acceptance and self-condemnation. Second, if whatever one "must" become or achieve isn't forthcoming, the individual sets himself or herself up to experience greater frus-

[3] Horney, K. *Neurosis and human growth.* New York: Norton, 1950.
[4] Ellis, A. The basic clinical theory of rational-emotive therapy. In A. Ellis and R. Grieger (eds.), *Handbook of rational-emotive therapy.* New York: Springer Publishing, 1977.

tration (see quote iii). Finally, absolutistic thinking restricts the student's range of choices and
sense of personal freedom (see quote iv).

As part of the process of developing a sharper awareness
of your own anxiety-producing mental activity, I strongly
suggest you perform the following "homework":

  i. Refer to your sheet from the exercise at the
     beginning of the chapter. Look over the thoughts
     and self-dialogue you wrote down and iden-
     tify each according to the ten categories just
     presented.
 ii. As you work on your next class homework assign-
     ment, keep a sheet of paper handy as you study to
     jot down interfering thoughts, negative self-talk,
     and worries.
iii. During your next quiz or test, "listen" to yourself
     for the occurrence of this negative self-talk and
     later record examples of it.
 iv. Review your written records to determine if
     there is (are) consistently recurring categories or
     content themes.

Managing Anxiety-Engendering Mental Activity

After detailing all of the brands of fear-producing and
disruptive mental activity characteristic of the academically
anxious student, you've probably developed an appreciation for how this kind of thinking whips up anxiety and
feelings of low self-confidence and futility. We shall take
the point of view that if it is possible to "talk" or think
ourselves into anxiety, perhaps it is possible to "talk" or
think our way out of panic or to keep anxiety at a tolerable

level. Psychologist Donald Meichenbaum[5] emphasizes that everyone, from time to time, engages in the self-defeating or illogical patterns of thinking outlined in the previous section. But what seems to separate the academically anxious student from the less anxious student is *how* each responds to or copes with those thoughts. The anxious student may respond to one negative thought by producing a whole string of catastrophizations and panicky self-talk (as does our Doonesbury cartoon character); or an anxious student will simply fail to challenge the questionable thinking and self-talk that results in greater academic stress. For example, note the difference in student coping styles in this academic situation:

Two studiers are burning the midnight oil to finish a math problem set for a 9:00 a.m. class. The assignment is tricky, and quite naturally feelings of frustration and anxiety tend to arise. Both engage in an anger-engendering comment reflective of their frustration. Note how the ineffective coper responds to this comment in a self-defeating manner.

Effective Coping Style	*Ineffective Coping Style*
"Drat. This math is a pain in the butt!"	"Drat. This math is a pain in the butt!"
↓	↓
Engages in a restorative self-dialogue to rekindle interest, reorient self to task, calm self down, and direct attention back on task:	Follows with 'Why' question: "Why do they make us do this garbage?"
↓	↓
"Whoa! Griping about math will only make me feel worse. Just	Engages in self-recrimination: "I should have started this assignment two days ago. I'll never learn!"

[5] Meichenbaum, D. *Cognitive-behavior modification.* New York: Plenum Press, 1977.

Effective Coping Style	Ineffective Coping Style
take it easy . . . Let's see if I can use some of that energy in a more constructive way to solve this equation . . . So far I've been hammering away using just one approach to the solution. Maybe if I do a little brainstorming, I can reach a solution from a different angle."	↓ Conjures up brief but vivid image of ultimate failure on the task. ↓ Engages in expressions of hopelessness and in negative self-evaluations: "What's the use? I could work on this all night and it wouldn't sink through my skull!" ↓ Experiences an increase in anxiety. ↓ Situation culminates in escape behavior—student leaves desk to perform other less demanding task.

At this juncture we are about ready to embark on assisting you to develop a new brand of inner speech that is incompatible with the old, anxiety-producing kind and to cultivate a personal language that restores a sense of emotional balance. But before we look at the specific coping responses, some points of emphasis are in order:

1. Typically, students resort to trite self-commands (e.g., "Don't worry"; "try to do your best") to cope with anxiety. Frankly, that is the kind of well-intentioned advice you're likely to hear from parents or relatives. But is it *really* what you would find effective for yourself? Might you want to apply a stronger or more creative self-communicative medicine?

2. As part of your self-change process, I urge you to evaluate critically and pick apart your anxiety-producing self-talk. What are the negative messages you use to "psych yourself down"? Hold them up to the light for inspection: are they valid? Do you really want to keep playing this baleful tape over and over in your mind?

3. Although I will provide many examples, it is important for you to generate *your own* inner speech, using language that is personally convincing to you, rather than copying me. Remember, the examples are only guides.

4. You will benefit greatly by *practicing* your new "script." Practice will help you become more adept at making a self-enhancing internal dialogue a more natural part of your style.

5. Finally, I strongly recommend activating your new "script" as soon as possible following awareness of mental activity of the negative kind. Quick application is advised because it is so easy to get caught up in a deteriorating downward spiral from which it becomes difficult to extricate yourself. The earlier example of the ineffective coper illustrates this problem.

Coping Response #5: Disrupting Negative and Critical Self-Statements and Unfavorable Comparisons to Others

Example #1

Negative self-statement: "I'm so slow, how can I even expect to pass?"

Disputation: "There I go again, running myself into the ground and predicting the worst. I'm tired of giving myself zero credit and automatically rating myself below everyone else. Besides, even if I were the slowest person on earth, berating myself isn't going to help me. Instead of the self-criticism, maybe changing my behavior would be better— like reducing my anxiety to increase efficiency and allowing myself more time and expecting less rapidity."*

Example #2

Negative self-statement: "Like with my last test, it was so hard it was a joke, and it got to the point where I didn't even care. Just write anything down. Just get it over with. That's how I know I'm a quitter."

Disputation: "Wait a minute . . . calling myself a quitter is making a pretty strong statement. Does my performance on that test prove me to be a quitter? Can I say on the basis of one exam that the best adjective to describe my psychological makeup is 'quitter'? Actually, when I think about it, I threw in the towel that day because I felt it fruitless to persevere in such an absurdly difficult test. Now, if I had the test to take over again, I'd do some things differently, like maybe take time to collect my thoughts, use some task-orienting self-directives to talk myself into a better mind-set, or ask the professor what she meant on a couple of questions."

---

*Please note: On paper these disputations appear rather time-consuming, but with practice it becomes possible to flash the gist of the countermessages through one's consciousness in only a few moments.

Example #3

Unfavorable comparison: "They say in design class you're supposed to learn from other students, but when I see what everybody else is doing, I feel bad because I couldn't come up with those ideas myself."

Disputation: "It probably makes sense that I don't come up with their ideas, because every student operates out of his or her own creative frame of reference. And besides, duplicating their designs isn't the point anyway; it's being able to incorporate some of their *insights* into my own work. Perhaps I haven't hit upon a satisfying design because I pay too much attention to what my neighbors are doing."

Example #4

Unfavorable comparison: "The fellow I studied with knows everything. Next to him, I really know nothing."

Disputation: "Hold it right there, old buddy . . . granted, he is sharp, but if I give up too much of my power to him, I'll only feel weaker and more vulnerable in comparison. Although it would be nice, I doubt I need his encyclopedic knowledge of the subject matter to get by on the test."

Let me point out several qualities inherent in these disputation examples and the coming coping responses:

   i. The examples strive to be *personally convincing.*
      If you use the same worn-out phrases to try to

BRANDS OF DISRUPTIVE SELF-TALK

calm yourself, you won't listen to them. It's best to use a creative, personalized dialogue with yourself. At this moment I can almost hear some of you saying: "But I'm not creative! I can't think of anything good!" Balderdash! That's just more negative self-statements and whining. As you can see, the examples presented use a vocabulary and style of reasoning that's within the grasp of most students.

ii. The examples reflect an *aggressive* tone. I recommend a dash of aggressiveness since the mental activity being disputed tends to overplay weakness and incompetence.

iii. The examples adopt a *realistic* perspective. It would be equally unwise to pump your self-esteem up with bogus claims such as "world's greatest student." I recommend searching for the truth of the matter, for what seems to be a plausible interpretation of the situation, and for realistic steps and suggestions to set the problem straight.

iv. The examples imply the desirability of taking *personal responsibility* for putting one's emotional house in order. After all, if I personally don't take specific steps (like providing myself with suggestions for coping behaviorally with frustration or disputing my negative thinking) to manage my emotions, who else will?

Before moving on to the next coping response, return to the examples of negative and critical self-statements and unfavorable comparisons to others listed in the previous section and apply your own creative, convincing disputations to them.

Coping Response #6:
Countering Anger-Engendering Self-talk

Example #1

Anger-engendering self-talk: "Chemistry sucks!"

Countermessage: "Hey, wait a minute! I realize chemistry is no fun, but if I keep ranting and raving about it, I'll turn it into an even greater pain in the neck. Since studying chemistry is such a burden, that's all the more reason to get it done quickly so I can go to something more enjoyable."

Example #2

Anger-engendering self-talk: "I hate it when all of your grade depends on just a couple of lousy exams!"

Countermessage: "If this issue of grading and evaluation really conflicts with my personal philosophy of education, maybe I'd benefit by explaining those views to the teacher. Perhaps I can explore the possibility of doing a paper or project to substitute for one exam or to supplement my test score grades."

OR

Alternative: Ask yourself what might be your underlying special meaning behind the grade. How has the grade in this course taken on so much importance? Does this appear valid in light of our discussion in Chapter 3?

Example #3

Anger-engendering self-talk: "I turn my papers in on time, but half the class manages to wheedle extensions out of the instructor. Can you blame me for being teed off?"

Countermessages: "Rather than stewing about my not liking two sets of deadline policies in this class, I'll express my observations to the teacher. Perhaps there are others in class who share my views and who can join me in talking with the teacher. This certainly is a more constructive approach than bellyaching to everybody about unfairness. Of course, if we do talk to the teacher, it will be preferable to present the facts in an appropriate fashion rather than griping indignantly to him."

OR

"I'm glad I don't resort to scams and excuses like these other people do. I'm satisfied with taking responsibility for getting my work in on time. What is distressing is the fact that I allow other people's behavior to have such an impact on me. I mean, just because people choose to act in a manner that's not really my style doesn't have to make me see red. That's nuts! I would rather choose not to let others exert that kind of influence over my emotional life."

Coping Response #7: Addressing "Why" Questions

Example #1

"Why" Question: "Why do they have to schedule tests one on top of the other?"

Addressing "Why" question: "Who knows why? They just do . . . But look: if I'm really straining under the load, perhaps I can request a makeup exam or extension in one course to ease the pressure."

Example #2

"Why" Question: "Why did I even decide to go pre-med?"

Addressing "Why" question: "Good question . . . sometime when I have about a month to spare I'll devote all that time to answer just that question."

OR

"Is that a legitimate question, or am I just blowing off steam?"

Example #3

"Why" Question: "Why don't these concepts stick in my head? Why isn't it clear?"

Addressing "Why question: "If I'm not grasping this material, that certainly is a problem. Perhaps applying some task-orienting self-directives (TOSD's) at this point will help organize my thinking and get me on track: Just relax a moment . . . Take another brief look over the section . . . Formulate in your mind what it is specifically that doesn't seem to be registering . . . If the subject matter still doesn't get any clearer, maybe calling a classmate for help or asking the instructor tomorrow will be better alternatives than making myself upset with these whiny 'Why' questions."

Coping Response #8:
Reanalyzing "What if . . . ?" Thinking

I highly recommend that this kind of catastrophic thinking be vigorously confronted and reanalyzed, especially since virtually any such worry can cause much undue concern. Three interchangeable variations on this coping response are described below.

A. Psychologist Arnold Lazarus[6] suggests placing the single word "so" in front of the "What if . . . ?" That little word puts the worry in quite a different perspecitve. Try it with these examples:
So . . .
. . . what if my best isn't good enough?
. . . what if my roommate aces the exam and I louse it up?

B. A second method of draining off some of the power of "What if . . . ?" thinking is to spell out for yourself some coping possibilities that can be employed even if the dreaded situation materializies. Going beyond the actual worry by reminding oneself of the coping choices available is an important step: too often students only verbalize the worry and get stuck at that point. Curiously, although their worries can be imaginative and graphic, students all too rarely exploit this creativity to manufacture coping scenarios. Furthermore, having in mind various coping strategies affords some sense of control or mastery over the situation that is incompatible with anxiety.

[6] Lazarus, A.A. *Behavior therapy and beyond.* New York: McGraw-Hill, 1971.

Example:

"What if . . . ?" thinking: "What if I am handed the exam and 'block'?"

Reanalysis: "That might just happen, and in the event it does, let's figure out how I would proceed at that point: first, I'd be on guard for any self-talk that would stir me up into a greater state of panic. I'd begin giving myself some instructions to stay on task and to reread the question s-l-o-w-l-y. I'd also relax physically and give myself a few moments to collect my thoughts and brainstorm for an answer. Failing that, I'd turn to a question I could answer since that would boost my confidence and get me absorbed in the test."

C. In Chapter 3 we outlined some of the presumed payoffs of worry. Sometimes it helps to analyze "What if . . . ?" thinking in terms of the "gains" to be achieved through worry, to ask oneself if the payoffs are really worth the price of worry. These examples illustrate the usefulness of thinking through some of the bonuses one may accrue from worry. When you become aware of the presence of "What if . . . ?" thinking, you may want to pause and aggressively pick apart the inappropriate uses of worry in order to help set yourself straight.

Example #1

"What if . . . ?" thinking: "What if I turn in the paper and it doesn't have enough references?"

Reanalysis: "That seems to be a reasonable worry, but I don't want to get fooled by it. I can easily use this worry as a convenient excuse to keep checking more and more references so that the paper will never get done. Of course, as I perform this "research overkill," I can rationalize that I'm working and involved, but that's really a sham . . . Actually, it's an excuse for avoiding the work and letting myself get immobilized by details."

Example #2

"What if . . . " thinking: "What if my final exam grade turns out as bad as my grades on the midterms?"

Reanalysis: "That's certainly an unnerving thought. But how am I helping myself when I get myself provoked by such a worry? Am I somehow expecting that this will motivate me to study harder for the final? I doubt that, since I already planned to devote considerable review time to it. More likely, this worry will make me overly sensitive to the test and that will have a demotivating effect on me!"

Coping Response #9: Attacking Absolutistic Thinking

We've already fingered absolutistic thinking as one of the prime culprits among our varieties of anxiety-producing mental activity. There are any number of ways to attack absolutistic thinking. I'll present four tips for helping you to undercut this pernicious thinking. In the examples that follow, watch how I incorporate these tips into my attack on the absolute statements. Again, the goal is to aggressively rethink these absolutes in order to gain more personal freedom.[7]

Tips for attacking:

i. Look critically at the statement. Absolutistic thinking is usually based on questionable assumptions about oneself and one's relation to the world. Does this statement make sense? How is it true? Where's proof to support it?

ii. What might be the implications of the absolutistic statement? If you were to adopt this mode of thinking what might be the effect on you personally?

iii. Beware of confusing *desirability* with *necessity*. Absolutistic verbs (must, got to, ought) imply "need." Frequently, academically anxious students get in a bind by telling themselves they desperately "need" to achieve a particular personal goal or situational outcome. They believe those goals to be necessary because failure to achieve them is considered worse than awful. Absolutistic thinking based on "need" leads to a slavish pursuit of goals and allows for no deviation. But are the goals and outcomes necessary or merely desirable? Will failure to achieve them

---

[7] For a thorough and practical treatment of correcting erroneous thinking styles, especially of the absolutistic kind, I encourage the interested reader to consult A. Ellis and R.A. Harper, *A guide to rational living*, Hollywood, Calif.: Wilshire, 1972.

lead to personal ruin? These are questions you will want to address in order to feel less constricted and entrapped by absolutistic thinking.

iv. Note the demanding tone inherent in absolutistic statements, especially the "should" variety. What actually start out as personal preferences become easily turned into behavioral and environmental demands—an insisting that oneself, other people, or one's environment be, act, or think differently. But to what extent can we expect our environment to accommodate to our demands? Are we setting ourselves up to experience immobilizing anger or hurt if the demands aren't realized? Who's to say things "should" be different than they are?

Example #1

Absolutistic thinking: "I can't accept myself if I do less than what I expect of myself. I've got to be perfect."

Strategies for attack: "Hold on . . . I know quite a few people who appear able to accept *their* mistakes and shortcomings. Is it really a question of my being unable to accept myself as less than perfect—or is it because I *won't*? Are there any natural laws requiring behavioral perfection? None that I know of, and that I require it of myself indicates I'm making some unrealistic demands on myself. Furthermore, if I do operate out of this belief, I'd likely be in constant tugs-of-war with myself, alternating between self-acceptance and self-condemnation, depending on how my performance is evaluated."

Example #2

Absolutistic thinking:　"I can't afford to screw up the exam. I've got to pass. There's no two ways about it."

Strategies for attack:　"I'm telling myself that I need to pass, that otherwise I could not endure the consequences. But this is really not true. Not passing means some frustration, inconvenience, and expense, but not personal destruction. What I really mean is that passing the test would be nicer, more desirable—but not an absolute necessity. Necessity means I'll be driven to succeed, which is just the sort of thinking that is incompatible with a relaxed, controlled approach to my work."

Example #3

Absolutistic thinking:　"I shouldn't be so slow . . . It shouldn't have to take me so much time!"

Strategies for attack:　"I'd *like* the studying to progress faster, but probably for a number of reasons that faster pace is not likely to be achieved. It doesn't make sense to demand a faster pace than I'm capable of performing and then to heap scorn on myself for not achieving it."

Example #4

Absolutistic thinking: "The university ought to wake up and start rewarding the teachers instead of the researchers."

Strategies for attack: "I would *like* the university to reward excellent teaching, and I would support such action. But *ought* the administration 'wake up' and change their policy? No, they don't have to. They're free to make their own decisions and to stand by them. However, my *demanding* this behavior from them is foolish on at least two counts: first, it's unrealistic to expect that the administration will respond to my dictating policy to them, and second, my demandingness could lead to such a feeling of anger against the 'system' that I won't be in a receptive frame of mind to tackle my work."

Coping Response #10: Calming Self-Dialogue

This coping respose is utilized to counter panicky self-talk ("Oh, Godisms") and panicky behavior. Calming self-dialogue is a set of special self-instructions geared toward reducing emotionality and reorganizing your behavior. Its purpose is not to leave you perfectly anxiety-free but to reduce emotionality enough to allow for more effective functioning. Calming self-dialogue can be coupled with rapid relaxation exercises (to be covered in Chapter 6). Again, let me emphasize two points: we want you to develop *your own* convincing dialogue that fits your unique style; and it is important that you *consistently apply* this dialogue, repeating as needed as panicky thoughts and undue emotionality arise.

Example #1

Panicky self-talk: "Oh, God! Now I'm getting nervous. Just what I need!"

Calming self-dialogue: "Instead of using the nervousness as a signal to go to pieces, use it as a cue to relax . . . you can deal with the nervousness . . . Take a moment to relax and slow things down . . . " (pause to relax).

Example #2

Panicky self-talk: "I'm supposed to be trying to study, but I can't even read the words because I'm so freaked out!"

Calming self-dialogue: "O.K. . . . just pause for a second . . . it's more important to calm down than to force the reading . . . (pause to relax) . . . now just take the words one at a time."

Example #3

Panicky self-talk: "There isn't enough time! There's still so much I don't know!"

Calming self-dialogue: "O.K., it's time to start talking to yourself again . . . No need to panic . . . no need to begin rehearsing for tragedy . . . take a deep breath and count down from 10 . . . Good . . . now relax and take things one step at a time."

Example #4

Panicky self-talk: Student sees classmates turning in test papers early and interjects: "Good Lord, how can they be done so soon?"

Calming self-dialogue: "Whoa! Take it easy! Don't start jumping to conclusions about what geniuses these people are . . . Just keep attention on your exam . . . Forget everybody else . . . Remember no negativisims, just stay on the task at hand rather than on worries."

Coping Response #11:
Thought-Stopping and Competency Imagery

Earlier in this chapter we discussed how mental images of anticipated troublesome situations or regretted past events can readily evoke feelings of panic and vulnerability. If we go by the adage that one picture is worth a thousand words, these frightening mental images can be especially anxiety-provoking. Coping Response #11 is suggested for two reasons: (a) we want to quell these disturbing images as soon as possible, for if allowed to run on in one's consciousness for too long, the resulting negative effect is hard to undo; and (b) after the frightening image has been put to rest, it is sometimes helpful to engage in an alternative, competency kind of imagery that can restore one's sense of personal confidence.

Example #1: Implementation of thought-stopping procedure

Since this thought-stopping procedure can be quickly applied, it is recommended for use during exams in order to disrupt the continuity of frightening mental imagery.

Jerry was hunched over his calculus exam, stumped for how to proceed. His first response after experiencing this setback was to let his mind wander off to a vivid recollection of his "choking" on some previous tests, in particular an economics test from last quarter. As he dwelt on this image for a few moments, he felt increasingly shaken. Fortunately, before he became too anxious he used his awareness of the upsetting image and his increasing emotionality as signals to apply the thought-stopping procedures:

    i. To himself, he shouted the word: "Stop!" He then embellished this command by simultaneously imagining a gigantic stop sign topped by flashing red lights and by pretending to hear the squeal of car brakes. This procedure effectively interrupted the frightening image.

    ii. Jerry next emitted task-orienting directives (see Chapter 4) for getting himself back on task ("O.K., if the problem is too tough, move on to the next one you know you can answer.").

    iii. He repeated these two steps as needed whenever the disruptive imagery recurred.

Example #2: Thought-stopping combined with competency imagery

This procedure takes a little more time to perform, and thus you may find it more useful prior to exams or while studying. However, once you've achieved some proficiency with the procedure, it could become part of your coping repertoire during exams as well.

Lynn was scheduled to take the Graduate Record Examination. A couple of days before the exam she had a series of unsettling images in which she saw herself walking into the large, impersonal auditorium, seeing the test booklets being distributed, hearing the serious proctor read the formal set of instructions, and then seeing herself becoming demoralized by it all. After dwelling on these disquieting images for a while, she began feeling weak and shaky. The next time she focused on this series of images, she responded with thought-stopping and competency imagery so as to bolster her feelings. She followed these steps:

i. As soon as she was aware of the frightening image and the accompanying negative emotional arousal, she performed the thought-stopping procedure. She shouted the words: "Hold it!" to herself and emphasized the command by mentally picturing a policeman with drawn gun halting a fleeing suspect. That put the disturbing set of images to rest.

ii. Next, in order to restore her senses of self-confidence and strength, she envisioned a competency image: a confident seamstress, Lynn imagined herself at her sewing machine, recalling how she had recently tailored a smart-looking outfit, one that required expert stitching and button-holing. She also recalled her friends' enthusiastic comments when she wore the outfit to a party. Lynn focused on this competency image until her feeling of confidence in herself was restored.

To implement your own thought-stopping and competency imagery:

i. Become aware, as early as possible, of the emergence of upsetting visual imagery and its accompanying emotional arousal.

ii. Use this awareness as a signal to employ the thought-stopping response: use a sharp, quick self-command to "stop!" the frightening image and use some other exaggerated cue to emphasize stopping (flashing red lights, railroad crossing gate and bell, factory whistle, policeman gesturing for traffic to halt, etc.).

iii. For competency imagery, select an activity that you have performed in an exemplary or masterful fashion. Bring this competency image into such clarity that you can vividly recall the specifics of the situation and the positive feelings of that moment. For example, some of my musically inclined counselees can recall performing a piece with utmost grace and style and can revivify the feelings of mastery and control that accompanied the performance. Other students recall moments from atheletic competition or successful interpersonal situations (such as winning an argument or debate) or performing with ease and confidence hobbies such as sewing, woodworking, or animal training.

iv. Be advised that repetition will be necessary. Unsettling imagery is likely to return; hence, reapplication of these procedures is urged. However, to the extent that you consistently and creatively apply this coping response, the frightening images should lessen in frequency and intensity.

Coping Response #12:
Employing Simple Self-Reminders

Sometimes it is necessary only to remind yourself that you have begun to engage in self-defeating mental activity (or task-irrelevant behavior or misdirected attention, for that matter) in order to jog yourself back on track. Self-reminders are yet another way in which one can keep maladaptive responding in check. Self-reminders may take such a straightforward form as:

> "There you go again . . .
> . . . comparing yourself unfavorably to others."
> . . . daydreaming instead of focusing on the book."
> . . . responding to frustration by predicting failure or tragedy."
> . . . putting extra pressure on yourself with those absolutistic should's and must's."
> . . . getting yourself upset with one worry on top of another."

Often the simple self-reminder is sufficient to disrupt worrisome thinking, negative self-dialogue, or other anxiety-producing mental activity; if not, stronger coping responses can be subsequently applied (e.g., task-orienting self-directives, reanalyzing "What if . . . ?" thinking, attacking absolutistic thinking, calming self-dialogue).

Homework

The next few paragraphs are probably the *most important* of the chapter, since the focus is now on applying this information. By now you have a solid appreciation for the fact that one's thoughts and self-talk have a direct bearing on emotions: academically anxious students can literally talk and think themselves into emotional upset. Hence, we've discussed eight coping responses as cognitive antidotes to this poisonous thinking style. However, gaining fluency with the coping responses will require *practice* on your part. Your goal will be to develop a new personal dialogue or "internal script" to restore emotional balance and to "deautomatize" your habitual anxiety-producing mental activity. Why is practice so important? First, it takes a little thought to fashion self-talk that sounds convincing, and it takes a dash of creativity to choose the precise words to get across to yourself the intended anti-anxiety message. Second, it takes *practice* to acquire a fluency with self-restorative inner speech so that it is at your disposal for quelling anxious arousal and upsetting thoughts during stressful academic situations.

The following suggestions may help you adapt the coping responses to match your particular style:

i. Refer to your written examples of your anxiety-producing mental activity. Now *write out* personally satisfying responses to them. Use the chapter examples as guides, but make sure your responses are phrased in your own language.

ii. Go ahead and phrase your responses as outrageously convincingly as possible. It doesn't hurt to use eye-opening or "grabbing" language. Remember, your coping responses are successful *only* if you *hear* them.

iii. Try your hand at writing rational arguments or disputations to some of your personal examples of absolutistic thinking or erroneous "If . . . then" conclusions. Aggressively punch holes in the "logic" behind this kind of thinking.

iv. After writing down your responses, practice saying them to yourself. In a sense, you're like an
actor learning new lines of dialogue. By silently
repeating them to yourself, they are more likely
to start feeling a natural part of yourself and to
become a part of your self-communication repertoire. Also, as you become more and more adept
at your coping self-talk, you probably will find
that the entire message need not be repeated to
yourself, but that a few key words or ideas will do.

In Chapter 8 we shall bring these coping responses and
all the others into a unified system for coping with
academic anxiety.

Summary

A strong case can be made for the argument that during
stressful academic situations academically anxious students
generate varieties of thoughts and self-talk that adversely
affect performance and increase emotional upset. In fact,
it is not so much the kind of academic situation that is
responsible for anxiety as it is what one *tells* oneself about
it.

The first half of this chapter contained detailed descriptions and examples of ten kinds of disruptive mental
activity common to academically anxious students. The
purpose of the descriptions was to increase awareness so
that you can quickly identify the emergence of thoughts
and self-talk that will prove maladaptive. Exercises to help
build this awareness were suggested. Specifically, the
reader was urged to begin listening for and recording his
or her own examples of anxiety-engendering mental
activity.

A major point of the chapter was that if one can think and talk oneself into an anxious state, it seems reasonable to use these same thought and self-talk processes to reduce anxiety to a manageable level. Moreover, clinicians and counselors have observed that what appears to separate the academically anxious student from the less anxious student is how each chooses to respond to negative thinking. To ensure more appropriate reactions to negative thinking so that sufficient emotional balance can be restored, eight coping responses were described:

     i. disputing negative and critical self-statements and unfavorable comparisons to others,
    ii. countering anger-engendering self-talk,
   iii. addressing "Why" questions,
   iv. reanalyzing "What if. . . ?" thinking,
    v. attacking absolutistic thinking,
   vi. calming self-dialogue,
  vii. thought-stopping and competency imagery,
 viii. employing simple self-reminders.

It was stressed that these coping response examples were to be used primarily as guides and that the reader was encouraged to fashion his or her coping responses using personally convincing and relevant language. Again, practicing this new restorative dialogue was recommended in order for it to become a natural part of one's cognitive repertoire.

CHAPTER 6

Physiological and Emotional Distress

Introduction

Some years ago, two psychological researchers, R.M. Liebert and L.W. Morris[1], identified two distinct components of a test anxiety reaction—emotionality and worry. Chapter 5 familiarized you with many types of responses subsumed under the worry component— panicky thinking, negative self-statements, "What if . . . ?" thinking, and so on—that academically anxious students emit under stress. The emotionality component consists of both the *emotional symptoms* of academic anxiety (described as feelings of panic, uneasiness, or "freezing") and the *physiological symptoms* caused by activation of the sympathetic division of the autonomic nervous system. The sympathetic division readies the body for action by

[1] Liebert, R.M., and Morris, L.W. Cognitive and emotional components of test anxiety: A distinction and some initial data. *Psychological Reports*, 1967, 20, 975–978.

increasing heart rate and blood pressure and by releasing sugar into the bloodstream.

From their review of research studies, Zung and Cavenar[2] have identified a broad array of symptoms found in anxiety disorders, many of which are common to academic anxiety. Although there is a wide variety of symptoms of emotionality, usually only a few are especially relevant for an individual at a given time. Below are the various categories and selected examples of each:

> *Affective (Emotional) Symptoms:* apprehension, uneasiness, helplessness, anticipation of danger.
> *Somatic (Bodily) Symptoms:*
> Musculoskeletal system: tremor, tension headache, muscle tightness, weakness, neck and back pain.
> Cardiovascular system: palpitation, rapid heartbeat.
> Respiratory system: hyperventilation, dizziness, feeling of choking, shortness of breath.
> Gastrointestinal system: nausea, vomiting, diarrhea.
> Genitourinary system: increased desire to urinate.
> Skin: face flushed, sweating.
> Central nervous system: insomnia, lack of concentration.

Psychologists who have studied academic anxiety reactions have obtained some surprising research findings concerning emotionality. Believe it or not, it was discovered[3]

---

[2] Zung, W.W.K., and Cavenar, J.V. Assessment scales and techniques. In I.L. Kutash and P.B. Schlesinger (eds.), *Handbook on stress and anxiety.* San Francisco: Jossey-Bass, 1980.

[3] Holroyd, K., Westbook, T., Wolf, M., and Badhorn, E. Performance, cognition, and physiological responding in test anxiety. *Journal of Abnormal Psychology,* 1978, 87, 442–451.

that high-anxious students are no more physiologically aroused under test conditions than low-anxious students. Holroyd and his associates found virtually *no* difference during a test simulation between high- and low-anxious students on such measures as heart rate and skin conductance (perspiration makes the skin a better conductor of minute quantities of electrical current). Furthermore, Morris and Liebert[4] found that the worry component usually interferes more with test performance than does emotionality. So how does it happen that emotionality becomes a problem? Why do so many academically anxious students report experiencing so much debilitating arousal? These questions require a little explaining.

Physiological and Emotional Distress: What Can Go Wrong?

As research evidence accumulates, it is becoming clearer that physiological symptoms are *not* the main problem. Most of the common academic anxiety symptoms are relatively minor and are more annoying than anything else. A more likely source of the problem is the *attention* paid to emotionality. Obviously, if attention is directed to the bodily symptoms, concentration is diverted from the academic task and performance will suffer. However, the problem is more than just misdirected attention. When academically anxious students attend to their symptoms, they *overestimate* the intensity—more intense emotional arousal is perceived than actually exists. It is what we tell

---

[4] Morris, L.W., and Liebert, R.M. Relationship of cognitive and emotional components of test anxiety to physiological arousal and academic performance. *Journal of Consulting and Clinical Psychology,* 1970, 35, 332–337.

ourselves about the emotionality—how we perceive it and interpret it—that is important. Our Chapter 2 case example illustrates this point: when Brian experienced a surge of emotionality during the exam, he interpreted it as a loss of control, a danger sign. The result of this interpretation was an increase in anxiety and a more panicky approach to the test. In effect what psychologists are learning is that the emotional and bodily symptoms are not the real culprits; rather, panic and poorer performance result because students attend too much to the symptoms, overestimate their intensity, and interpret emotional arousal as a distress signal.

Over twenty years ago, two psychologists, Richard Alpert and Ralph Haber[5], distinguished between two types of interpretations that students make of emotionality. Some people interpret anxious emotionality as *facilitative* (helpful) to performance. For example, these students claim that nervousness spurs them on to better performance, that the pressure of deadlines brings out the best in them, or that the challenge of a hard test is welcomed. Other students react to the same level of anxious emotionality by labeling it as *debilitative* (harmful) to performance. These individuals report that nervousness detracts from performance, that they can get so nervous about a test that they eventually don't care how well they do on it, or that being unable to answer questions at the beginning of a test is so upsetting that performance on later questions is adversely affected.

Besides paying undue attention to emotionality, overestimating its intensity, and misinterpreting its meaning, a fourth problem frequently occurs: students apply the

[5] Alpert, R. and Haber, R. Anxiety in academic achievement situations. *Journal of Abnormal and Social Psychology*, 1960, 61, 207–215.

wrong measures to cope with it. For example, during an exam students may try to ignore their emotional and bodily symptoms and push themselves to work or concentrate harder. Then what happens is that the tension builds until it reaches crisis proportions. By then it's too late to take simple measures to deal with it. Or students might tell themselves to relax (which isn't always sufficient to reduce emotionality) without practicing some actual relaxation procedures. They figure that during a test they shouldn't waste time relaxing.

A Plan for Chapter 6

A main point of this chapter is that it is not so much the emotionality or physiological arousal that is critical, but rather *how one reacts to it*. What do I mean by that?

One positive way, as we have seen, to react to anxious emotionality is to "read" it as being facilitative: that is, its presence might be regarded as evidence that one is gearing oneself up to tackle a task or to rise to the challenge. Another positive way to react to anxious emotionality or to the bodily symptoms of anxiety is to consider their presence to be *signals to engage in coping responses*.

We have already discussed a number of coping responses, which you have probably guessed could be easily adopted to minimize the unsettling effect of emotionality. For example:

i. *Calming self-statements* (see Chapter 5), spoken to oneself in a soothing manner, can help to induce a more relaxed state.
ii. *Redirecting attention* (see Chapter 4) can be employed to turn attention away from bodily symptoms and onto the task at hand.

iii. *Task-orienting self-directives* (see Chapter 4) can help you get more absorbed in the academic task and consequently less involved in self-concerns.*

Now in Chapter 6 we shall focus on *three relaxation procedures* to quell emotionality. The plan is to let the presence of symptoms associated with anxiety act as signals for you to respond with various kinds of relaxation. The first relaxation coping response, Rapid Relaxation, is a relatively simple, easy-to-apply technique for use especially during exams. A second relaxation coping response, Deep Muscle Relaxation, can be employed outside of class, typically after studying or during academic preparation. Moreover, once you've become proficient with Deep Muscle Relaxation, elements of it can be applied during in-class evaluation situations as well. The third relaxation coping response, Relaxing Imagery, is to be used following Deep Muscle Relaxation. Relaxing Imagery, a kind of "mental relaxation," provides students with a respite from the busy, planful, stress-producing train of thinking that often occupies their attention.

Coping with Disruptive Emotionality

There are many relaxation methods. Some people swear by a tub of soothing warm water. Some flee their noxious environments for unpopulated hiking trails. Others rely on chemical means (alcohol or tranquilizers) to achieve relaxation. In this section we shall assist you to acquire several kinds of relaxation skills: rapid relaxation for specialized use during examinations; deep muscle relaxation to relax

---

*Such adaptations of coping responses as well as the systematic application of multiple coping responses are addressed in Chapter 8.

the body; and relaxing imagery to help you momentarily shut down that incessant stream of pulsating mental activity.

Coping Response #13: Rapid Relaxation

You don't need to be as limp as a dishrag while taking an exam. Being able to keep emotional arousal at a manageable level is usually sufficient. The goal is for you to become adept at rapid relaxation, a technique involving slow, deep breathing which, if practiced properly, can help you achieve a reduction in emotional symptoms. Rapid relaxation won't leave you perfectly relaxed, but it can quell arousal just enough to keep you functioning effectively.

I recommend rapid relaxation for use during exams, especially during the first 5 to 10 minutes when emotionality is peaking. Also rapid relaxation can be utilized during studying/exam preparation or during those stressful minutes while you wait for the start of an exam.

Here are the steps involved:

   i. Decide to take a few moments away from the exam. This is of basic importance. Sometimes students figure that they can't lose any precious time.

   ii. Close your eyes. As you sit in your exam seat or work chair, tense all your muscles. Really try to "scrunch up" as many muscles as you can.

   iii. Once you've tensed the muscles, take a deep breath (inhaling through the nostrils) and hold your breath for a count of five (keeping your muscles tensed all the while).

   iv. After reaching the count of five, simultaneously

exhale rapidly through your lips and quickly let go of your muscle tightness by silently telling yourself: "Now relax."

v. With eyes still closed, go as limp in the chair as you possibly can after relaxing.

vi. Now with muscles relaxed, take a second deep breath through the nostrils. Hold this breath for a couple of seconds. Then *slowly* exhale through the lips.

vii. As you exhale, repeat the word "calm" to yourself. You'll probably repeat "calm" 7 to 10 times while slowly exhaling.

viii. Repeat these steps once or twice to achieve greater relaxation. Each application takes about 30 seconds.

With regard to rapid relaxation, please bear in mind these points:

i. Rapid relaxation is best initiated immediately upon awareness of unsettling emotionality (the feeling of clutching or panicking) or of the bodily symptoms of anxiety.

i. It is far better to use this technique than to try harder to concentrate and resist the tension.

iii. Rapid relaxation is a skill to be learned, and like other skills, it requires practice to perfect.

iv. Set aside about 10 uninterrupted minutes during the day to practice this coping response.

v. Also, get some practice while studying in your work chair. Take your attention away from your book and go through the eight steps. The more diligently you practice, the easier it will be to utilize rapid relaxation during academic evaluations.

Coping Response #14: Deep Muscle Relaxation

Coping Response #14 is a technique specifically designed for relaxing the musculoskeletal system. After an evening of studying or a full day of classes, you may want a technique to help you relax physically. Learning deep muscle relaxation has its benefits: since physical relaxation is a state that is incompatible with anxiety, it actually doubles as an effective anxiety control procedure; also, once you learn deep muscle relaxation, you can take this skill out into your daily routine—upon recognizing the existence of bodily tension, you can quite inconspicuously relax those muscles and subsequently move about your environment in a more relaxed manner. I'll have more to say later in this chapter about how to generalize deep muscle relaxation to other situations.

The technique of deep muscle relaxation (also called progressive relaxation) was pioneered over fifty years ago by the physiologist Edmund Jacobson. His original relaxation regimen was exceedingly thorough and time-consuming. Over the years, his technique has been modified to focus on a relatively small number of key muscle groups. Deep muscle relaxation is now an almost standard technique taught by mental health professionals, physical therapists, and physical education instructors.

The essence of deep muscle relaxation involves first tensing and then relaxing in sequence each of the various muscle groups. These tensing/relaxing phases serve several purposes:

i. Intentionally tensing muscles and studying the feeling that results fosters awareness of what muscles feel like when they are tense. This is important because many individuals proceed through the day oblivious to the muscle tightness that is building in their bodies.

ii. Tensing and relaxing fosters a second kind of awareness, namely the qualitative difference between what muscles feel like when tense and how different they feel (in a positive way) when relaxed.

iii. The goal of the relaxation portion is to leave that particular muscle group feeling more relaxed than before it was tensed.

iv. Fundamentally, deep muscle relaxation strives to develop a greater sensitivity to the body. Becoming attuned to bodily tension is important, because this awareness of tension can be used as a signal to take corrective action (e.g., initiate a relaxation coping response).

Preparation for practicing deep muscle relaxation. Since deep muscle relaxation may be new to you, several points are needed to familiarize you with the proper approach to it:

i. *Frame of mind:* decide to take the time to practice relaxation. The purpose of relaxation is compromised if you feel the need to rush through it. Instead, consider relaxation to be a special time for you, a time for self-improvement, a time for enhancing your feelings of well-being.

ii. *Where:* most any comfortable surface will do such as a bed, recliner, or carpeted floor. Recline with legs uncrossed and arms at your side. Choose a room free from distractions and of an agreeable temperature. Be comfortable—remove shoes, glasses or contacts, and loosen tight clothing.

iii. *How long:* deep muscle relaxation takes about 20 to 30 minutes.

iv. *When:* time of day is pretty much up to you. Some people prefer to practice during mid or early evening. Others choose late afternoon after classes. Many prefer to perform deep muscle relaxation in bed prior to falling asleep.

v. *Why practice:* like any other skill, learning relaxation requires practice. Practice is the ticket to developing a keen sense of body awareness. Moreover, once you achieve proficiency you can reach the point where first tensing the muscles is no longer necessary—you may need only to focus attention on a particular muscle group and suggest to yourself that those muscles relax. But practice is required to achieve this more sophisticated skill level. We'll cover this abbreviated focusing/relaxing method at the end of this section.

vi. *How much practice:* generally 5 to 7 sessions per week for 2 to 3 weeks is enough to become quite proficient. Some people learn faster; others need more time. As I mentioned in point v., an abbreviated relaxation method can be initiated once the deep muscle tensing/relaxing phase has been mastered.

vii. *Be advised:* carefully study *ALL* the steps and directions that follow *BEFORE* trying it!

Tensing exercises for muscle groups. These exercises follow a fairly standard progression from arms to legs. Stay with this sequence until you become familiar with it; later you can rearrange the exercises to suit your preference. As you read, try out each exercise to get a feel for the instruction. Just tense the particular muscle group for a few seconds. Don't get into the full-fledged relaxation process yet. By the way, as you go through this informal practice, try to tense just the muscle groups in question and not the rest of your body.

Hands and arms

1. *Dominant* (right hand if you are right-handed) *hand and forearm*. Make such a tight fist that your fingernails almost dig into the palm of your hand. Your hand may tremble as you tighten, but that's O.K. Next, curl your fist in toward your forearm, as if trying to touch your knuckles to your forearm. Notice the tension across your knuckles and back of your hand and through the wrist. Feel the uncomfortable tightness in the muscles of your forearm.

2. *Dominant arm biceps*. Make a biceps muscle, bending your arm at the elbow. Leave your hand *open* (remember, you're tensing just the biceps). Be aware of the escalating tightness and tension as the biceps muscle balloons.

3. *Nondominant hand and forearm*. Repeat as in Step 1.

4. *Nondominant biceps*. Repeat as in Step 2.

5. *Triceps*. While keeping your back against the surface on which you are reclining, extend your arms outward or upward, palms up. Pretend you are pushing with all your might against an imaginary wall. Notice the tension in your triceps and through your arms.

   As you worked your way through these steps, I hope you remembered to tense *only* those muscles specified in the exercise. Keep the rest of the body as relaxed as possible.

Face

6. *Forehead*. Tense the muscles of the forehead by trying to raise your eyebrows up to your scalp line. Be aware of the furrows of tension across your forehead.
7. *Midface*. This exercise is best described as making a "prune face." Close your eyes hard. Now "scrunch" up the muscles around your eyes and wrinkle your nose. Observe how the tension manifests itself through your face.
8. *Jaws and mouth*. Clench your teeth together. Now draw back the corners of your mouth into an exaggerated smile. Expose as many teeth as possible. Feel the tension in your cheeks and jaw and the tightening of muscles down the sides of your neck.

Neck and Upper Body

9. *Neck and shoulders*. Attempt to touch your chin to your chest. (Careful! This exercise is easy to overdo.) Feel the muscles in the back of your neck tighten.
10. *Shoulders*. Lift up your shoulders, trying to touch them to the tops of your ears. Feel the discomfort across the top of your shoulders.
11. *Shoulders and chest*. Pull your shoulders back, as though trying to touch your shoulder blades together. Tune into the tension across the chest and shoulders.

Midbody

12. *Stomach.* Pull in your stomach muscles as far as possible as if trying to touch your bellybutton to your backbone. This is the tensing you would perform if you expected a punch to the stomach. Again, notice how the resulting tension manifests itself.

Legs and feet

13. *Thighs.* Simultaneously tense your thigh muscles. These muscles are the heaviest and thickest of the body, so give them a vigorous flexing.
14. *Front of calf, right leg.* Push your toes forward as far as possible, keeping your heel anchored to the surface on which you are reclining. (Don't overdo it, because calf muscles cramp easily.) Feel the tightness produced in the back portions of your calf and around the ankle.
15. *Front of calf, left leg.* Repeat as in Step 14.
16. *Back of calf, right leg.* Again keeping heel anchored, bring your toes backward so they point toward your face. Notice the tension produced in your lower leg.
17. *Back of calf, left leg.* Repeat as in Step 16.
18. *Right foot.* Curl up the toes of your right foot by trying to bring them under the sole of your foot. (Not too strenuously, since cramping could result.)
19. *Left foot.* Repeat as in Step 18.

Instructions for tensing and relaxing. The aims of the tensing and relaxing phases are to increase awareness of: (a) what tension feels like; (b) which muscles experience tension; (c) the qualitative difference between tensed and relaxed muscles.

The procedure usually involves these several steps:

i. Inhale deeply and then immediately tense the particular muscle group quickly and vigorously, but don't tense so hard that you cause pain.

ii. Hold the tension (and your breath) for 5 to 7 seconds. Carefully study how the tension feels and where you experience it.

iii. Exhale and immediately let the muscles relax. Relax them quickly. Let the muscles go as limp and relaxed as possible. Notice the feeling associated with the loosening up and relaxing of the muscles. Relax them for 20 to 30 seconds.

iv. Inhale and tense (for 5 to 7 seconds) the same muscle group a second time.

v. Exhale and relax. Allow about 45 seconds for recovery from the second tensing.

vi. After you've completed all 19 tensing steps, check your entire body for any muscles that still feel tight. Gently retense and relax them.

vii. After completing Step vi, you've probably achieved about as deep a state of muscle relaxation as is possible for this particular practice session. Even though you may not be perfectly relaxed, take 1 to 2 minutes to enjoy the relaxation you have attained.

One of the principal factors in successful muscle relaxation is an effective script of self-instructions to induce tension and relaxation. What you tell yourself while proceeding through the exercises can help you to: (a) develop a smoother practice cadence or rhythm; (b) achieve a more vigorous muscle tension; (c) attain a deeper level of muscle relaxation; and (d) become more aware of the feelings produced in the muscle groups. Using Step 1 (dominant hand and forearm), I'll illustrate the kind of self-instructions appropriate for each tensing/relaxing phase. Study them closely. For each of the other eighteen steps, you can make the necessary modifications, such as substituting the name of the next muscle group. You can silently repeat these instructions to yourself; or perhaps better yet, you can tape-record your own instructions and play them for your practice sessions:*

"Take a deep breath and hold it . . . Now quickly ball your right hand into a tight fist and curl it in toward your forearm . . . Really tense those muscles . . . Study how the tension feels, how the skin stretches across the knuckles, how the tightness feels in the forearm [Hold for 5 to 7 seconds] . . . Exhale and now relax . . . Let go of the tension as quickly as possible . . . Really let those muscles loosen up and relax . . . Let the relaxation spread through the entire arm . . . Notice how different the muscles feel as they become relaxed [Relax for 20 to 30 seconds] . . . Now *inhale* and *tense* again . . . Again, notice where the tension makes itself felt [hold for 5 to 7 seconds] . . . Now exhale and relax . . . Let those muscles unlimber . . .

** Some students prefer a professionally recorded cassette tape. A number of relaxation tapes, containing comparable training exercises, are available at modest cost. Two I can recommend are obtainable from:

Self-Management Schools
745 Distel Drive
Los Altos, CA 94022
(Tape composed and narrated by John Marquis, Ph.D.)

Cybersystems, Inc.
4306 Governors Drive, West
Huntsville, AL 35805
(Tape developed and recorded by A. Jack Turner, Ph.D.)

Really let them go . . . Just let a wave of relaxation come over them . . . Appreciate the difference between the feelings of tension and relaxation . . . Spend a few seconds enjoying the relaxation and warmth that are spreading through these muscles [Relax for 45 seconds after the second tensing] . . . [Proceed to dominant arm biceps]."

In order to add some variety to your set of self-instructions, you can incorporate some of these phrases for:

Tensing	Relaxing
"Be an observer of the tension."	"Feel how the relaxation flows."
"Feel where the muscles stiffen."	"Just let the feeling of relaxation radiate through the muscles."
"Try to make the muscle tighten. Push it to the limit."	"Let the muscles go completely limp, limp like a puppet whose strings have been cut."
"Hold that tension. Really tune into how it feels."	"Let a wave of warmth and relaxation take over."
"Inhale and tighten."	"Relax quickly. Relax completely."
"Focus on those sensations of tightness."	"Enjoy the relaxation."
	"How different the muscles feel now . . . so relaxed."

After you have gained proficiency with deep muscle relaxation. After about two to three weeks of practice, most people reach a level of proficiency where relaxing can be achieved without first tensing each muscle group. To perform this abbreviated *focusing/relaxing* muscle relaxation:

   i. Begin in the usual comfortable, reclined position.

  ii. Focus your attention first down to your feet. Merely *suggest* to yourself that your feet begin relaxing. You can use the familiar self-instructions to suggest looseness, radiating warmth, and welcome relaxation.

 iii. Work up through the body—calves, thighs, stomach, chest, shoulders, arms, neck, jaw, face, forehead—focusing attention on each muscle group and achieving relaxation through suggestion.

 iv. If you feel some tension in any particular muscle group, just tense and relax that one muscle group.

  v. After achieving a relaxed state, spend several minutes enjoying this experience.

 vi. Again, this abbreviated method is *not* recommended until you have developed familiarity with the entire tensing/relaxing exercises.

Generalizing deep muscle relaxation to exam situations. Proficiency with deep muscle relaxation yields two other bonuses. First, there is the obvious connection with Rapid Relaxation (Coping Response #13): students trained in deep muscle relaxation can achieve a relaxed state more quickly after exhalation. Also, possession of a finely tuned awareness of the existence of muscle tension has its benefit. For example, if during an exam you notice the appearance of muscle tension, you can quickly relax it away before it becomes too disrupting. The recommended procedure is to tense that particular muscle group and then quickly release the tension and let those muscles relax as completely as possible. Keeping your body relaxed can help you keep academic anxiety at a tolerable level.

Coping Response #15: Relaxing Imagery

Practicing deep muscle relaxation provides you with a method for quieting tension in the musculoskeletal system: the experience of deep muscle relaxation is incompatible with being physically tense. Now that you can relax your muscles, we shall introduce you to a coping response for bringing relaxation to your mind. The same principle of incompatibility applies here: we want a mental relaxation response that cannot simultaneously coexist with the usual anxiety-provoking, unsettling, busy mental activity that incessantly clutters our consciousness. As one student put it: "I spend the day planning how to get everything done, worrying about what I'm going to say in a paper, and whether I'll be ready for upcoming exams. I even take all this to bed with me. It's always hanging over my head!" The aim of Coping Response #15 is to provide an intentional respite from this ongoing, wearisome welter of mental activity.

Coping Response #15 is a follow-up procedure to deep muscle relaxation. Relaxing Imagery is a nice "finishing touch" to deep muscle relaxation since both mind and body are becalmed. The steps involved in Relaxing Imagery are as follows:

   i. Perform the now familiar deep muscle relaxation. Use the standard tensing/relaxing exercises; or if you've already gained proficiency with them use the abbreviated focusing/relaxing method described in the last section.

  ii. After establishing deep muscle relaxation, let your relaxing image emerge in your consciousness. (What constitutes the relaxing image is described below). Picture this image in your mind's eye as vividly as you can. Try to project yourself into the scene. Choose an image that involves as many sensory modalities (sight, smell, etc.) as possible— that helps to absorb you in the image.

iii. From time to time extraneous or intrusive thoughts will interrupt your relaxing image. That's to be expected. When that happens, merely acknowledge that your attention has been diverted and calmly return to the image. Even over a five-minute span, you may experience a good many intrusive thoughts, so be tolerant of them. The goal, remember, is *relaxation*, and an angry or impatient response to the mental intrusions sabotages the relaxation.

Designing your relaxing imagery. My experience is that students usually choose imagery from one of three themes: *nature, relaxing activity,* or *fantasy.* Some examples can give you guidelines for designing your own relaxing imagery. Read each example through. Choose which of the three themes (or one of your own) seems right for you. Spend some time creating your imagery—write it down, choose descriptive vocabulary, and mentally rehearse it until it seems suited for eliciting in you a deeper level of relaxation.

Nature: Typical scenes include being on the beach or seashore, in the forest, in a flowering garden, or sitting under a tree during a spring rain. One student generated the following seashore image that she found particularly relaxing:

"In my mind's eye I can see the long, unpopulated stretch of reddish sand on the familiar beach on Prince Edward Island. It's where we used to go for summer vacations. I've spread out a blanket, and I stretch out on it. There's hardly a cloud in the sky. The sky is a brilliant blue—so clear and blue that I feel enveloped by the radiance of the day. I feel the warmth of the sun on my shoulders and how the sun raises a film of perspiration on my skin. The sun shines hot, but now and then a breeze stirs that blows cool and refreshing. I sense that unmistakable seashore tang in the air, a smell that's a mixture of salt water and marine life— kind of salty, kind of fishy, but very pleasant. Above me several gulls glide through the sky, and I can hear their cries rising and falling with the sound of waves rolling onto the shore."

Note: This student chose a familiar scene that readily yielded a strong, peaceful image. Note also her use of each of the senses, which helps involve her in the scene.

Relaxing Activity: A wide variety of such images are possible: woodworking, piano playing, walking the dog, or fishing in a babbling stream are a few that students have chosen. One young man's relaxing activity image involved driving his new car. Just how this activity acquired relaxing qualities is described by him as follows:

"What I visualize is a stretch of the highway from campus to my home. I've driven it many times, and I know it like the back of my hand. The highway is flat, an easy drive. I can see the roadside scenery flash past me—farmfields, trees, billboards. Traffic is always light. I can feel that it's just me, the road, and my new car. I can clearly see myself in the car—the dash-board instrumentation, the console. I have a feel for the steering wheel and the feel of the car on the pavement. I've got some soft music on the stereo that's helping me cruise along. I can even smell the new car 'aroma.' What I'm also aware of is being filled with a sense of pleasant anticipation, like everything is right with my world because I'm heading home and getting away from the hustle and bustle of school. I'm going home to relax, and I can feel that the pressure's off."

Fantasy: Some effective imagery can be completely make-believe, but if you can get caught up in its dreamlike flow of events and get involved in its curious or interesting quality, it can prove very relaxing. For example, after practicing deep muscle relaxation, this young woman entertained an absorbing cave fantasy, which is imagina-tion of the purest kind since she'd never set foot in a cave:

"In this fantasy I see myself exploring one of the wooded hillsides near my home. In a tangle of under-brush I see rocks and some tree limbs that seem to be covering a kind of entranceway into the side of the hill. When I clear away the rocks and branches, to my amazement I discover an entrance to a secret cavern. I decide to enter. There's a natural rock staircase that I descend leading down and down into the earth's crust. A fantastic natural fluorescence lights my way. What opens up before me is an under-ground panorama of beautiful stalactite and stalagmite formations—all in rich earthtones of red, yellow, and brown. I can feel the coolness and damp of this underground world. From high above me I hear the dripping of tiny rivulets of water cascading down the rock. I can also discern a lilting, whistling melody as the wind spirals through the columns of mineral formations. I continue on my exploration. After walking some distance, I come upon an open area that contains heaps of precious stones. The light reveals gleaming mounds of sapphires, emeralds, and diamonds. I run my hand through this treasure, and the gems blend together in a kaleidoscope of color."

Summary

Two distinct components of a test anxiety reaction have been identified: worry and emotionality. Worry consists primarily of cognitive interference of the kind detailed in Chapter 5. Emotionality consists of both emotional symptoms (e.g., apprehension, "clutching," uneasiness) and bodily symptoms (e.g., muscle tightness, stomach upset, sweating).

Contrary to popular thinking, emotionality does not exert as much of a negative influence on academic performance as does the worry component. In fact, on measures of physiological arousal during test simulation, high- and low-anxious students are virtually indistinguishable. However, emotionality can prove troublesome to academic performance when students:

(a) pay undue attention to it,
(b) overestimate its intensity,
(c) interpret it as having a debilitating effect,
(d) fail to employ appropriate methods to control it.

In this chapter several relaxation methods were described for effectively reducing emotionality:

Rapid Relaxation (Coping Response #13) was recommended for use during examinations. The presence of emotional or bodily symptoms was to be used as a signal for employing Rapid Relaxation. Early detection of symptoms and swift application of Rapid Relaxation were suggested in order to keep emotionality from getting too far out of hand.

Detailed instructions were provided for learning *Deep Muscle Relaxation* (Coping Response #14). This technique can be used outside of class, such as during study breaks or after studying. Once proficiency with Deep Muscle Relaxation is achieved, one becomes more aware of the presence of bodily tension. This relaxation skill can be generalized into exam situations so that during tests muscle tension can be spotted and inconspicuously relaxed away.

Relaxing Imagery (Coping Response #15) is to be performed after achieving deep muscle relaxation. Relaxing Imagery, a kind of "mental relaxation," involves becoming absorbed in a vivid but pleasurable mental image. Dwelling on this refreshing or restorative imagery affords a mental vacation from the busy, planful, and stress-producing mental activity that so often crowds one's consciousness.

It was also stressed that these relaxation techniques, like any other skill, require practice in order to become effective.

CHAPTER ◇ 7

Inappropriate

Behavioral Patterns

Introduction

When students are faced with an academic situation that they interpret as threatening, we have seen that several things can go wrong:

—attention is sidetracked onto internal or external distractors;

—one's thinking process is interfered with—instead of task-directed thinking, disruptive, anxiety-producing mental activity is generated;

—emotional and physiological symptoms occur, which, depending on how students react to them, can negatively affect performance.

Now we encounter a fourth category: *behavioral patterns* that work against students during exams or academic preparation. These inappropriate or maladaptive behaviors

161

feed back into the whole picture of academic anxiety, reinforcing feelings of lack of control and reducing performance effectiveness. In this chapter we shall discuss three broad, overlapping categories of problem behavior patterns—

> panicky behavior
> immobolization and avoidance
> procrastination

—and suggest coping responses that can be brought to bear against them.

What Can Go Wrong: Panicky Behavior

Sometimes test-takers' overt (observable) behaviors give them away as the anxious ones. Take Neil, for example, as he was taking an open-book, open-notes exam:

> If you were observing Neil, you'd be struck by his uncoordinated efforts and restlessness. He looked out of control, leafing wildly through his notes in search of some elusive fact, furiously chain-smoking cigarettes, and fidgeting in his chair. Panicky behavior was Neil's most visible problem. But he was also experiencing some other difficulties: he was having a hard time focusing on the question at hand without thinking about upcoming questions (the problem of task-generated interference), and he was muttering to himself several expressions of hopelessness and futility.

Sometimes one's test-taking and studying styles take on, like Neil's, a panicky or frantic appearance. This panicky behavior may result from a sense of urgency about the completion of a task or from a belief that speediness is a desirable way of coping under pressure. Of course, panicky behavior can feed right back into a general feeling of being overwhelmed by the situation.

Becoming aware of your overt panicky behaviors gives you yet another clue that it's time to start coping. Coping Response #16 is intended as an alternative to panicky behavior. Later in this chapter we will discuss several other coping responses that can be adapted to quell panicky behavior. As you read them, think about how they could be so applied.

Coping with Panicky Behavior:

**Coping Response #16
(Acting Under Control)**

One of the best ways to gain control over panicky behavior is to *act* under control. That's right, Coping Response #16 suggests that you play-act the part of someone who is supremely confident. Acting Under Control has its benefits. First, a rather obvious benefit is that behavior settles down and you become a more efficient student. Second, calm, collected behavior can brake the snowballing effect of anxiety, which is especially important during exams.

The third benefit requires a little explaining. Regarding panicky behavior, frustrated students often tell me they can't help the way they act. "Look, I have such a lack of self-confidence and so many self-doubts that of course my behavior is going to appear disjointed and out of control. How could it appear otherwise with such attitudes?" Unfortunately, reforming attitudes can prove a lengthy process. To save wear, tear, and time, it can be more advantageous first to *change behavior* and then attitude change will follow. Psychologist Darryl Bem[1] reviewed studies on the relationship between attitudes, beliefs, and behaviors and found that attitude changes tend to *follow* rather than precede changes in behavior. Thus, as your behavior becomes more controlled, there may be a resulting change in self-attitudes toward greater assuredness and confidence. A nice benefit, indeed!

The instructions for acting under control are straightforward:

i. Assume the posture or behavioral set of a student who appears to everyone to be in absolute self-control. Perhaps you have a friend who looks cool as a cucumber when taking tests. Use that person as a model for your own behavior. Try copying the image that that person presents.

ii. Sometimes students express their futility through comments to friends and acquaintances about how hard a test or assignment is. Make an effort to cut down the frequency of these remarks and other types of whining or complaining.

iii. Slow down any franticness or speediness and assume a measured pace.

iv. Try on an unabashedly self-confident manner to see how it feels. It probably will seem artificial at first. That's to be expected. But you don't even have to be first fully convinced that it needs to feel natural—just play-act the role for a while. You may find that as you rehearse this new role, you will actually begin to grow into it.

[1] Bem, D.J. Self-perception: The dependent variable of human performance. *Organizational behavior and human performance*, 1967, 2, 105–121.

What Can Go Wrong: Immobilization and Avoidance

It often happens that a student's progress on academic tasks hits a few snags so that stuckness, immobilization, and avoidance result. Take a careful look at these examples. We'll refer to them later in the chapter.

Steve scheduled some library time to study reference sources for his paper on existentialism. But the first thing he did upon arriving at the library was to visit the student lounge area. There he found a few friends with whom he spent an hour socializing. When he eventually got to the stacks, some journals on human sexuality caught his eye. He looked these over for a while. By the time he located the philosophy shelves, it was already so late that he only had time to photocopy a couple of articles and check out a book. He figured he'd read those materials tomorrow.

Steve's situation reflects a common student problem: letting academic progress get stymied by *task-irrelevant* behaviors. Steve's socializing and titillating reading matter are irrelevant to the task at hand.

Joyce was doing well in all but one course, economics. She had hardly picked up the book all term. The graphs and terminology looked forbidding. She purposely shunned the book lest she discover that the concepts were beyond her comprehension. "I might start a chapter and find that I don't understand it at all," she claimed. For Joyce there are more "payoffs" for not tackling economics than there are for taking a risk with it. Such payoffs include: avoidance of the criticism she would direct at herself if her understanding of economics proved deficient, and avoidance of threatening "What if's" (e.g., "What if I'm not as smart as I thought?")

Joyce's stuckness relates to her adherence to Special Meaning #2 (see Chapter 3). She equates self-worth with academic performance to such a degree that failure to understand economics immediately prompts her to call her intelligence and personhood into question. No wonder she avoids the book!

During my sophomore year in college I roomed with an architecture student named Rick. Before Rick was ready to draw, he performed an elaborate preparation ritual. He swept eraser crumbs off the surface of his drawing board; adjusted and readjusted the overhead light, angle of table, and height of stool; lined up numerous pens and mechanical pencils, and so on. Finally after about 45 minutes the table would be set just right, and Rick would then excuse himself for a coffee break as a reward for all this "work." He'd return two hours later.

Rick had become a master at *self-deception*: he had fully convinced himself that his ritual was bonafide work. Worse yet, he rewarded himself after performing it. Rewards (coffee breaks or other pleasurable activities) are most effective *after* having accomplished some real work. After all, since reinforced behaviors stand a good bet to be repeated, we want the appropriate behaviors to be reinforced. By first rewarding himself with a coffee break for performing the empty ritual, Rick was unwittingly strengthening his own avoidance tendencies.

Carol was seated at her dorm-room desk intending to complete a three-page paper for her freshman English course. A short paper like this was due at the end of each week. "These are such dumb assignments," she said to herself. "I hate them. I can't ever think of a blessed thing to write!" While waiting for inspiration to strike, she phoned a friend to confirm a weekend ride home, recopied a couple of weeks' worth of biology notes, and balanced her checkbook. Not surprisingly, no spontaneous theme ideas came to her while she was engaged in these other activities. She was still stuck.

Carol's case illustrates immobilization brought on by anger-engendering self-talk and expressions of futility. This kind of mental activity interferes with an adaptive approach to the problem of writing the theme. To compound her stuckness, Carol engages in *parallel activities* (phone call, biology notes, and checkbook) that further deflect her from the relevant task.

Chris was struggling with the first question on his electrical engineering exam. It was a four-part question, with the answer of the first part required to figure out the other three parts. He made several stabs at answering the first part, but no solution was forthcoming. Feelings of anxiety and frustration mounted as time ticked away and he had little to show for his effort. Chris' feelings of anxiety and frustration should have been signals that it was time to move on to another question. But his response was just the opposite: he felt himself becoming irrationally determined to finish this question and was perplexed by his inability to let go of it. As he later explained: "I *had* to finish it! I can't cope with the idea of leaving something undone."

Chris' stuckness had a dual source. First, he chose the *wrong coping strategy* (pushing himself harder) in response to his anxious symptoms. He would have fared better had he relaxed and used some task-orienting self-directives to guide himself away from the question. Second, his *absolutistic thinking* style wiped out his behavioral options (he "had to" complete the question before moving on), thereby ensuring immobilization.

Coping with Immobilization and Avoidance

The previous section provides some clues as to *when* and *what kind* of problem exists. But the bigger question is what can be done about it? In other words, how can a student help himself or herself choose approach rather than avoidance behaviors? Move beyond a snag? Opt for responsibility rather than rationalization?

We have already seen that the special meanings students attach to academics make tasks harder than they really are, thereby increasing the likelihood of their being avoided. Also, students' negative and critical self-statements contribute to perceived low self-efficacy, and when students doubt their personal effectiveness, immobilization usually results. Hence, one solution is to aggressively challenge the thinking or "mind-set" behind the immobilization:

    i. *Attack absolutistic thinking:* A lot of stuckness can be traced to absolutistic thinking. Take the example of a student who struggles to write term papers. Each attempt at an introductory paragraph is discarded—it doesn't sound right or isn't what the student wants to say. Granted, the introduction may not be precisely right, but the key point is that as the rest of the paper develops it is possible to go back and revise. The student experiences stuckness because he or she demanded that "it's *got to* be just right" before moving on.

Returning to Chris' situation, he might ask himself: "Can't I *really* live with an incomplete answer? Does it make sense to demand completeness? Is it true that I don't possess the ability to loosen myself from a sticky test question? What's the result if I am inflexibly determined to finish everything I start?" As Chris questions his "need" for closure, he takes an important step toward personal freedom.

It's an ongoing process, this chore of getting oneself unstuck. Each time snags are encountered or progress is waylaid, it's important to listen to what you are telling yourself about the task. If you recognize any absolutes lurking about, then aggressive rethinking and attacking them are recommended for prying yourself loose from their grip.

ii. *Counter anger-engendering self-talk:* Carol's nasty remarks about her theme assignment may have been just "blowing off steam." Sure, it's fun to gripe, but these comments don't provide positive suggestions for coping with stuckness. Instead, might Carol have used her awareness of anger-engendering self-talk as a signal for choosing some self-directives to pull for creativity and a more flexible approach to the task?

iii. *Debunk specious personal meanings regarding academics*. One of Joyce's problems was that she let self-worth get bound up with understanding economics. She avoided the economics book lest its graphs and terminology prove unfathomable, from which she would conclude that she wasn't all she was cracked up to be. But does lack of understanding of economic principles prove that one's self isn't up to par? Is it wise to impart such significance to one course? What does poor facility with economics prove anyway? Does the failure to grasp economic graphs quickly expose a damnable deficit? Those are questions that Joyce failed to address. Had she thought them through, economics might have lost some of its threatening quality, and she would have found it easier to approach.

A second problem was Joyce's perceived low self-efficacy. Since she believed herself practically incapable of handling the subject matter, she avoided it. This compounded her stuckness.

iv. *Reconsider payoffs for avoidance*. Avoidance is a predominant style of many academically anxious students because there is "a method to their madness." Referring again to this chapter's case examples, consider these payoffs:

—avoidance for Steve meant reprieve from an undesired activity and a chance to do things that at the moment were more fun;

—avoidance for Joyce meant not having to take personal risk;

—avoidance for Rick meant the development of a successful self-deception system that he used to trick himself into believing this ritualized behavior was real accomplishment;

—avoidance for Carol was shirking an onerous task and feeling justified for doing so.

But notice that all these presumed payoffs reinforce escape, self-deception, stagnation, and safety. Each sacrifices long-term gain for a short-term fix. Do you want these short-term payoffs, or would you rather shoot for growth, accomplishment, and calculated risk?

As you are aware, these suggestions are based on coping responses covered in previous chapters. Next I shall recommend new measures to cultivate approach rather than avoidance behaviors and responsible action rather than immobilization. This section concludes with a discussion of four such coping responses.

Coping Response #17: Seeking Help

I marvel at the large percentage of students who routinely refuse to seek help even though it would make things easier for them. Often seeking help entails little more than asking a roommate, friends, or teaching assistant for tips in understanding a concept. If broader knowledge deficits exist, taking on a tutor is advisable. This might have been the most appropriate coping response for Joyce, our friend who kept economics at arm's length.

I don't mean that you should make a pest of yourself and run for help each time a problem develops, but availing yourself of others' assistance can help bring down some frustrating barriers to progress. If you refrain from seeking help, you might want to take a closer look at how you hold yourself back. If your situation is similar to that of my counselees, it could be that some absolutistic thinking and erroneous "If . . . then" conclusions are behind the inhibition:

— "If I ask someone for help, it's like copping out. I'll be too dependent on them next time."
— "I shouldn't bother anyone. They'll be annoyed if I approach them."
— "I'll took foolish by asking some dumb question. Anyway, you're supposed to figure these problems out by yourself."

Coping Response #18: Behavioral Rehearsal

Some years ago psychologist Ron Dubren developed a cigarette-smoking cessation and maintenance program. Part of Dr. Dubren's program involves helping recent ex-smokers rehearse appropriate responses to situations in which the temptation to smoke again would be very high. Dr. Dubren counsels that:

> "The goal of behavioral rehearsal is to put yourself into the imagined situation before it happens. For example, a week before a big party, you sit down and picture yourself already there. You see the people, the food and drinks, and of course, the smokers. You begin to feel the temptation to smoke. Now, by using behavioral rehearsal, you can also imagine yourself overcoming this temptation. You can see how, for example, you decide to go outside for a short walk or get a glass of ice water when the urge overcomes you. This kind of previous practice can be very helpful once you are in the real situation."[2]

[2] "The Quit-It Plan and Maintenance Program," copyright 1976 by Ron Dubren.

This Behavioral Rehearsal coping response can be applied very effectively to a wide range of academic problem situations. The concept is easy: simply envision a potential problem situation and how you would cope adaptively with it. It's a particularly appropriate strategy for Steve, the fellow who prefers socializing to reference reading. For Steve each trip to the library is an entry into a high-temptation situation, since he is likely to head for the student lounge. What might be useful for Steve is to project ahead to his next library visit and mentally rehearse handling the temptation to avoid the relevant task. Steve's rehearsal of this scenario might sound like this:

"Tonight I'll go the library to look up some term paper references. As I project ahead several hours, I see myself walking from my room across campus to the library. As I walk, I remind myself: No messing around. Get the references read *first*. Then head off and find your friends! I walk up the marble steps and through the heavy glass doors. I'm inside now and if I turn left and go downstairs, I'm in the lounge. The pull to the left is strong, like a magnet attracting me. But I see myself taking a deep breath and instructing myself to stay on course. At this critical moment, I decide to turn right—I'm heading for the stacks! Hooray! I feel I've won a battle with myself. Now I'll get my work done and then reward myself with time in the lounge."

Homework practice.   Many students fail to take advantage of this technique of projecting ahead and rehearsing coping responses to problem situations. Yet I think it is an extremely helpful approach. Before moving on to the next coping response, I want to recommend two "homework" exercises.

First, let's adapt Behavioral Rehearsal to the problem that confronted Chris—the difficulty in pulling away from the exam question. Use Behavioral Rehearsal to see yourself managing this problem. While performing this "dry run" rehearsal, see yourself utilizing various important coping strategies such as: (a) recognizing the signals to move on to another test question (signals like mounting frustration, meager answer yield given time spent on question); (b) performing task-orienting self-directives that suggest letting go and being flexible; and (c) using calming methods like Rapid Relaxation to counter interfering emotionality.

Second, now identify a relevant area of concern for you regarding avoidance or immobilization and rehearse your own behavioral coping solution to it.

Coping Response #19: The Premack Principle

Coping Response #19, termed the Premack Principle after the psychologist[3] who researched the phenomenon, is especially appropriate for dealing with avoidance, procrastination, and task-irrelevant behavior. This principle states that if Behavior B tends to occur more frequently than Behavior A, then the frequency of A can be increased by making Behavior B contingent upon it. That may sound somewhat complicated, but the basic idea is probably not new to you. To put it more simply, if you are more likely to play electronic games (Behavior B) than to study (Behavior A), your study time could be increased by making the

[3] Premack, D. Toward empirical behavior laws. I: positive reinforcement. *Psychological Review*, 1959, 66, 219–233.

games contingent upon first having performed some studying.

Proper application of the Premack Principle is incompatible with the shady deals some students strike with themselves—"I'll go to the lounge to meet friends, then go and study." If properly employed, the Premack Principle offers a legitimate payoff. Behavior B (the electronic games, for example) acts as a *reward* for first doing Behavior A (the studying). This task-relevant behavior-followed-by-reward sequence is the most desirable, since it is the appropriate behavior (studying) that is being rewarded. Recall from our previous chapter examples that this sequence was not followed. Steve performed his rewarding activities (socializing and reading) prior to studying; and Rick performed a task-*irrelevant* behavior (worthless ritual) followed by a coffee break reward.

Of course, the Premack Principle works only as well as you *honestly* put it into practice. You can easily sabotage its purpose, for example, by studying for only a brief period of time and then rewarding yourself with lots of an enjoyable activity. Hence it is advisable to combine the Premack Principle with:

i. Your own new internal dialogue that challenges, disputes, and questions the thinking that fosters avoidance.

ii. Behavioral Rehearsal (Coping Response #17) for practicing the implementation of the Premack Principle under problematic circumstances.

iii. Self-Reminders (Coping Response #12) in order to jog yourself back on task.

Coping Response #20: Negative Modeling

You can learn a lot just by paying attention to others. Watch friends who typically overstress themselves on academic tasks or who fall apart during exams. How do they fashion their own disintegration? How does their behavior look? What do they say about the academic task? You can use their experience as a kind of negative modeling*—they are exhibiting (or modeling) the sort of behaviors that are best avoided. In short, other people's maladaptive behaviors can be examples for how we don't wish to act.

If Carol had a roommate, the roommate might use her as a negative model. This hypothetical roommate might observe Carol and comment thus:

"Every time one of her crummy little themes is due, she starts griping. She goes: 'I can't think of anything. I don't have anything to write because I don't know what they're talking about in class!' Then she reaches for the phone and calls her boyfriend or does some other thing to put off writing the paper. She puts it aside for a while, but when she comes back to it, she gripes some more. I tell you, if I have themes to write next term, I'll get them done right off with as little complaining as possible. If I do have trouble figuring out what to write, I'll get help. Believe me, I've seen

* *Positive modeling* exists as well. With positive modeling, attend to other students who appear to function smoothly. Is there anything about their style you would like to emulate? Incorporating their smoothly functioning style into your behavior repertoire could be part of your Acting Under Control coping response (see #16).

how Carol has made her life miserable for herself—
and for me!"

What Can Go Wrong: Procrastination

Not uncommonly avoidance behavior becomes a habitual
and integral part of a student's life-style; it becomes
a personally acceptable way of coping with life's responsibilities, and it interferes substantially with one's personal
and academic effectiveness. When this happens, avoidance as a relatively brief diversion from task turns into
procrastination.

Procrastination is a complex phenomenon. But after
working with students on this problem. I've seen some
predictable patterns emerge. Let's look at four of them.

I. Procrastination is maintained by reinforcement.
Students may derive certain payoffs by procrastinating, but they are payoffs that usually turn
out to be self-defeating ones.
    i. One obvious payoff is the temporary relief
    experienced when an undesirable task is
    avoided.
    ii. Procrastination can be a nice face-saving
    excuse. If a student turns in a poor per-
    formance, it is easier to attribute failure to
    procrastination ("I waited 'til the last minute
    and didn't have time to do a good job") rather
    than to lack of ability.
    iii. Some students use procrastination to manip-
    ulate the "system." This is a powerful
    payoff. Students can parlay procrastinaation
    into extensions, incompletes, or other special
    considerations.

      iv. A few students find that procrastination provides a psychological thrill. It's exciting to see how close one can get to a deadline and still pull off the assignment.

  II. Procrastinators are masters at making academic tasks harder than they really are. We've already touched on several of these points:

      i. Procrastinators usually possess negatively skewed self-perceptions. They see themselves as not capable of meeting the challenge presented by the task. This may, in some circumstances, be an accurate assessment of the situation, but often the real problem is perceived low self-efficacy.

      ii. Procrastinators attach special personal meanings to academics that impart extra significance to tasks.

      iii. Absolutistic thinking predominates. For example, many procrastinators make perfectionistic demands that increase task difficulty.

      iv. Procrastinators tend to lump all outstanding tasks together, thereby allowing them to assume overwhelming proportions. So often I hear the complaint: "I've got biology to do, then chemistry, and a psych paper to write after that! How can I ever get it all done?"

 III. Procrastinators are masters at self-deception, and this feeds into the problem:

      i. One common example is the bogus deals that students make with themselves. The claim: "I'll start my math problem set after watching M*A*S*H" is a promise that begs to be broken.

      ii. Rationalizations are common: "I'll do my

anthro reading now, which is at least getting *something* done," even though researching a history paper is of more importance.

   iii. Procrastinators manage to limp along on good intentions. Elaborate daily schedules and routinely ignored self-imposed deadlines give students a fleeting sense of control.

IV. Procrastinators use emotions to work against themselves:

   i. Procrastinators rely on negative emotions— anger, guilt, anxiety—as motivators. These often exacerbate the problem: the disruptive mental activity associated with anxiety interferes with planful, creative, task-focused thinking.

   ii. Guilt is a common motivator as some students shame themselves into working. But what can happen is that after a student makes himself or herself feel lousy enough for a long enough period of time, a kind of penance is performed. In effect, wallowing in guilt for a while atones for the "sin" of procrastination. This procrastination/feeling guilty/guilt-serves-as-atonement process allows the student to "get off the hook," so to speak, and sets the stage for future irresponsible behavior. This guilt cycle may repeat when the next threatening academic task is encountered.

   iii. Procrastinators habitually use negative emotions and feeling states to deceitfully duck responsibility. "I'm too tense to get anything done now" or "I don't feel creative now" are common examples.

    iv. Because of the undone tasks hanging over their heads, many procrastinators do not enjoy their stretches of free time. Unfortunately, procrastinators get little relief: working is a chore and so is not working. Recuperative and relaxing off-time hours are often unavailable to them.

Coping with Procrastination

After taking into account these characteristics of procrastinators, I've designed Coping Response #21: Guaranteed Scheduling Technique (GST)[4] as a systematic intervention that addresses at least five areas of concern:

1. *The nature of the problem suggests a coping response that is flexible and realistic.*

   Procrastinators set unrealistic deadlines and draw up impossibly meticulous deadlines. GST involves a far more reasonable schedule that can become a natural part of students' everchanging routines.

2. *The nature of the problem suggests a coping response that teases out accomplishment.*

   Mastery and control over academics and feelings of satisfaction are achieved through task accomplishment. Once students approach and complete tasks, this sense of accomplishment is likely to increase motivation and sustain progress.

---

[4] For a detailed treatment of GST, the interested reader may consult Ottens, A.J. A guaranteed scheduling technique to manage students' procrastination. *College Student Journal*, 1982, *16*, 371–376.

Accomplishment serves as an appropriate, honest reinforcer. GST emphasizes *guaranteed* accomplishment and does not recognize good intentions, rationalizations, and bogus deals as being sufficient.

3. *The nature of the problem suggests a coping response that fosters self-awareness.*

We've already talked about the importance of your becoming a keen self-observer. This involves becoming aware of the brands of disruptive mental activity reviewed in Chapter 5. It also involves becoming aware of task-avoidant behaviors such as those described earlier in this chapter. The disruptive mental activity and inappropriate behavioral choices act as barriers to achievement. GST encourages you to challenge and dispute the negative thinking and to opt for adaptive behavioral choices.

4. *The nature of the problem suggests a coping response that helps make both off-time and on-time hours more productive.*

As pointed out before, procrastinators often don't enjoy their valuable off-time hours. Even when they are at their work stations procrastinators may be engaging in extraneous tasks that make their on-time hours less effective. GST emphasizes the importance of productive study time so that leisure time can be enjoyed without guilt or anxiety. Whether working or playing, the goal is to become as totally involved as possible in one to the exclusion of the other.

5. *The nature of the problem suggests a coping response that aims for consistency.*

I find that procrastinators' work habits can

fluctuate wildly. For example, a student might pull an all-nighter to prepare for a test and then, figuring a rest has been earned, "blow off" the next several days. In the meantime assignments pile up that then require another all-nighter, which results in several more days of "earned" vacation. GST strives to build more consistency into students' schedules so that these sapping fluctuations are minimized.

GST: How It Works. A daily contract is a central feature of GST. The following contract would appear at the top of an 8½″ × 11″ page:

> Date _____
>
> On this date I guarantee to myself that I will spend _____amount of time on relevant academic assignments. I have concluded that this amount of time (in hours) contracted for is reasonable and that I will use it productively. I shall also write down at the bottom of the contract page any thinking, worrying, or behaviors that I set up as barriers to my completing this contract, and I shall also write down how I attempted to overcome these barriers.
>
> Signed _____

You may wonder why I recommend a contract. I think a contract is more likely to keep students honest about meeting their academic responsibilities. Furthermore, a contract has an aura of "officialness" about it and compared to simple good intentions is less likely to be subverted.

Note some of the key words in the contract:

"Guarantee"—this word specifies actual completion of the contracted time and represents a serious self-agreement. It is less ambiguous than such wishy-washy terms as "try to," "intend to," or "get around to."

"Time"—you contract for time studied rather than an amount of work (number of pages read, problems solved). My experience is that an amount of work usually takes longer to complete than students estimate, and hence time can be easier to control.

"Relevant"—the most currently important academic work is to be tackled, not just those assignments that are easy or convenient.

"Reasonable"—it is important to contract for the most substantial amount of time that can be guaranteed to be carried out on the date of contract. Too often procrastinating students overestimate how much time they intend to study. Regarding contracted time, I suggest that 15 minutes of studying on a particular day is probably unreasonably short and 12 hours probably too long. I'll return to this issue of "reasonableness" later on.

"Productively"—work is to be carried out in an efficient manner. Time spent daydreaming or worrying at one's work station doesn't fulfill the contract. When daydreaming or worry interfere, it may be desirable to apply Coping Response #1 (Stimulus Control) in order to achieve more productivity.

A contract is to be drawn up for each day of the week, including weekends. *Consistent* daily accomplishment imparts a feeling of satisfaction and helps sustain motivation. I realize that occasional circumstances (e.g., illness, travel) will arise that preclude making a contract on some days, but keep those days to a minimum. (Check yourself for the excuses you use to avoid a daily contract.) I recommend that you draw up the contract either the night before or the morning of the date in question. Students wonder how much time to begin contracting for—that question of "reasonableness" again. Initially students are very enthusiastic about GST and draw up overambitious contract lengths. *Caution:* the contract calls for *guaranteed* time and not for how much time you think you *ought* to study. Before making a daily contract, survey your responsibilities for that particular day and contract for a length of time that is consonant with those responsibilities. Thus, a student who has no classes on Tuesday might contract for four hours of study time on that day; however, if the student has a full day of classes plus an extracurricular activity on Wednesday, he or she might contract for only one-half or more hour of study time.

To develop a sense of reasonable contract length, a charting system is helpful. For each day of the week record how many hours of study time were contracted for and how many hours you actually performed. A typical chart looks like this:

	Time Contracted For	*Time Actually Completed*
Monday	3½	2
Tuesday	2	4
Wednesday	1½	1
Thursday	3	3
Friday	1	1½
Saturday	5	4
Sunday	2½	2½

Disparities between the contracted and completed columns gives you a sense of the appropriateness of your contract lengths. Usually a week or two of charting is sufficient for this purpose. One additional note: unfortunately, no "banking" of study time is allowed in GST. That is, if you perform beyond your daily contracted time, you can't save the time and apply it to another day. I add this stipulation so that past accomplishments aren't used as justification for spending less time on upcoming academic responsibilities.

I mentioned earlier that I recommend students put in writing on the bottom of the contract sheet those mental or behavioral barriers that could interfere with the completion of their contract. This helps build awareness of such impediments as:

absolutistic thinking	task-irrelevant behaviors
worrying	permission-giving to avoid tasks (e.g., bogus deals, rationalizations)
negative self-statements	maladaptive special meanings attached to academics

On the same page, you're to document the coping response(s) you used to overcome these barriers. Write down *specifically* what you did or said to yourself as coping strategies.

This component of GST can be made clearer by the example of a senior English major who had been avoiding working on his honors thesis. On the bottom of his contract page he formed two columns to document his experience:

My barriers to getting the job done	*How I reorient myself*
1. I notice that I'm thinking: "He (my advisor) won't like	1. I remind myself that I'm worrying again, predicting

the looks of this chapter." As I think about this, I'm aware of a *strong* urge to put the work aside.

the worst. I take time to reanalyze this "What if" thinking. I tell myself: "This is just the first draft and my final grade isn't on the line. In fact, it would be helpful if this draft triggered a spirited response from him. That might give me some more insight into the problem."

2. As the day goes by, I become more concerned that everything I wanted to say about *As I Lay Dying* has been rehashed by other critics. I feel a sense of defeat—I'm going to have to start from scratch.

2. There I go again, letting the expressions of futility upset me. I remind myself of two important points:
   i. I'm responding over-critically to my thesis.
   ii. I'm overstressing myself with some absolutistic thinking—that my arguments *must* be perfectly new and supercreative.

3. Today's Sunday. It's my usual routine to buy a New York *Times* and spend a few hours with it. I feel a strong urge to buy a copy and get immersed in it. So much easier than struggling with the thesis.

3. I'm better off not using the *Times* as a task-irrelevant activity. In fact, if I buy it and start reading it now, I'll really be distracted. There's potential there for blowing off half a day. Remember, completing the contract is #1 priority. *After* I put in time writing the thesis, *then* I can read the *Times*—remember the Premack Principle.

There is one additional component of GST, a *reward component*. If you meet or exceed a predetermined number of time contracts in a week, I encourage you to reward yourself. This reward might be a desired tangible object (record album, book, or article of clothing) or a pleasurable activity (skiing, movie date, computer game). But this reward is available *only* if the requisite number of contracts is completed. You'll sabotage the effect of GST if you reward yourself noncontingently (i.e., treat yourself to the reward without first having achieved your weekly number of successfully completed contracts). I find that whatever the reward, students are more likely to enjoy it when it is earned through honest contract completion. Regarding the reward component, my experience is that successful completion of four of seven contracts per week in order to obtain a reward is a good place to start. The number usually presents a fair beginning challenge for most procrastinating students.

Some final thoughts about GST: if you plan to adopt GST to combat a procrastination problem, I *strongly* recommend following the procedures *to the letter*. Draw up copies of the contract. Set reasonable daily goals. Do the charting. Become aware of your procrastinating style. Document on the bottom of the contract page your barriers to completing the contract and the coping strategies you used to overcome them. Set up a reward system.

What can happen is that students, thinking they understand the ins and outs of GST, start cutting corners. This almost always yields poor results. For the first few weeks, "go by the book." After you've gained familiarity with GST, you can perhaps abbreviate it. Also, the purpose of GST is to improve your effectiveness, not to achieve perfection. Even if you go by the book, there will be days when you backslide—intentionally don't make a contract or revert to your old procrastinating style. Backsliding doesn't mean you've failed and must abandon the technique. Take the backslide in stride and go back to GST the next day. Try to learn from the backslide and apply that knowledge to your next contracting day.

Summary

Maladaptive behavioral responses are an additional component of an anxiety reaction. Academically anxious students behave in ways that exacerbate the situation.

Panicky behavior, the observable, frantic-looking behavioral concomitant of anxiety, is one common problem. Coping Response #16 (Acting Under Control) was suggested as a countermeasure to panicky behavior.

Immobilization and *avoidance* are other behaviors that characterize the academically anxious student. Several brief case examples were presented that described relatively typical ways in which immobilization and avoidance are manifested. Some general coping suggestions were given that were adapted from previous coping responses. Four new coping responses were introduced: Seeking Help (#17), Behavioral Rehearsal (#18), Premack Principle (#19) and Negative Modeling (#20). Suggestions for implementing each were provided, using the case example illustrations.

The complex phenomenon of procrastination and its dynamics were discussed. Coping Response #21 (Guaranteed Scheduling Technique) was designed to take into account the dynamics behind procrastination and to act as an effective means of combatting the problem. The various components of GST and instructions for its implementation were presented. It was recommended that if students initiate GST as a coping response, they closely follow the procedures in order to ensure better success with it.

CHAPTER ◇ 8

A Model for Coping

with Academic

Anxiety

Introduction

We have reached the eighth and penultimate chapter. I congratulate you for having hung in this far with me. Pretend I'm pinning a gold medal of commendation on you!

Over seven chapters we've covered quite a bit of territory. Just to refresh your memory, we have seen that certain characteristics or symptoms are common to academic anxiety:

Misdirected attention and attention-focusing difficulties
—interfering external distractors (noise, social-evaluative cues)

—interfering internal distractors (task-disruptive thoughts, physiological and emotional distress)
—task-generated interference
—reduced cue utilization

Anxiety-producing, disruptive mental activity
—panicky self-talk ("Oh, Godisms")
—"Why" questions and "If only" statements
—negative and critical self-statements
—unfavorable comparison to others
—anger-engendering self-talk
—evocation of frightening mental images
—erroneous "If . . . then" conclusions
—absolutistic thinking

Physiological and emotional distress
—emotional symptoms (panic, uneasiness, "clutching")
—physiological symptoms (bodily changes associated with anxiety such as muscle tension, perspiring)

Inappropriate behaviors
—panicky behaviors
—immobilization and avoidance
—procrastination

Maladaptive coping choices
—waiting too long before initiating coping procedures
—use of weak, stereotypical, noncreative coping procedures
—use of negative emotions (guilt, anxiety) to motivate oneself
—pushing oneself harder instead of relaxing

Negative interpretation of events
—symptoms of anxiety (e.g., emotionality, panicky behavior) are labeled as distressing or debilitating

—frustration, setbacks, or mistakes are seen as indicators of danger
—unacceptably low evaluation outcomes are interpreted as threatening to self and leading to catastrophic consequences

Special meanings that contribute to making academic work more threatening
—if the academic situation is seen leading to an unfavorable outcome, then cherished plans may not be realized, and that would be terrible
—if one's performance, evaluation outcome, or ability level is less than acceptable, then one is less acceptable as a person
—if one's academic standing isn't up to par, then one risks losing the esteem, respect, or approval of important people
—if one's academic standing isn't up to par, then significant others will have cause to be emotionally upset

These, then, are the characteristics of academic anxiety that we have been working to modify or minimize. We've also developed twenty-one coping responses for managing academic anxiety. Now we shall see how various coping responses can be employed to combat the different anxiety symptoms. In this chapter we shall experiment with *combining* coping responses. By combining coping responses we can achieve a more powerful, multimodal, and creative attack against the symptoms of anxiety.

The Plan for Chapter 8. I have three goals for this chapter. First, I shall introduce you to a general model for coping with academic anxiety. Second, I'll explain the rationale behind each phase of the model. Finally, I'll include a number of examples to illustrate how the model works.

Coping with Academic Anxiety: A Model

In my counseling work, I like to use a four-stage model for conceptualizing how to cope with academic anxiety. Take a careful look at it:

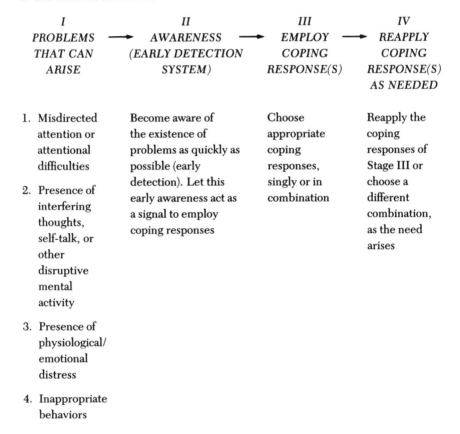

I PROBLEMS THAT CAN ARISE	II AWARENESS (EARLY DETECTION SYSTEM)	III EMPLOY COPING RESPONSE(S)	IV REAPPLY COPING RESPONSE(S) AS NEEDED
1. Misdirected attention or attentional difficulties 2. Presence of interfering thoughts, self-talk, or other disruptive mental activity 3. Presence of physiological/ emotional distress 4. Inappropriate behaviors	Become aware of the existence of problems as quickly as possible (early detection). Let this early awareness act as a signal to employ coping responses	Choose appropriate coping responses, singly or in combination	Reapply the coping responses of Stage III or choose a different combination, as the need arises

The arrows signify a dynamic process, with one stage leading to another.

Stage I.   By now you have a pretty solid familiarity with the types of symptoms common to academic anxiety.

Hence you know specifically *what* can go wrong. We've also seen *when* these symptoms are likely to occur (to review, refer to Chapter 5 for our discussion of the four general stressful situations). These anxiety symptoms occur singly or in clusters, usually in clusters. Thus, during an examination or while studying, a student may simultaneously experience shifts in attention, rising emotionality, and interfering thoughts. A key point is that if these symptoms aren't checked, the end result may be increasing anxiety (remember the "snowballing" effect) and reduced performance effectiveness.

Stage II of our model is predicated on three important concepts. The first concept points to *awareness* as a condition for producing change. What are we doing (or failing to do) that culminates in intolerably high levels of anxious arousal? Obviously in order to rectify a problem, we wish to be aware of what is going wrong.

The second concept is the importance of *early* awareness. Early detection of the symptoms of anxiety and quick ameliorative action are the keys. One common mistake is that students wait until they are very upset before initiating coping procedures. By then they are in a panic state that requires an inordinately long time to subdue. Recent research in the field of behavioral medicine beautifully illustrates the usefulness of early detection training. After recognizing the early signs that *precede* epileptic seizures (e.g., headache, ringing in the ears), patients are able to take corrective action to prevent seizures or to diminish their severity.[1] For example, one young man

---

[1] Zlutnick, S., Mayville, W.J., and Moffatt, S. Modification of seizure disorders: The interruption of behavioral chains. *Journal of Applied Behavior Analysis*, 1975, 8, 1–12.

could sometimes stop the seizure progression by talking to himself, telling the seizure to: "Get out of here." A woman was reported to be able to stop a seizure by performing an incompatible behavior, namely shaking her head vigorously from side to side.[2] The principle behind our general anxiety control model is essentially the same: become quickly aware of the early signs of anxiety—the feelings, thoughts, behaviors, and attentional shifts—that can sabotage effectiveness and escalate into full-blown panic; and then choose coping procedures that prove incompatible with the symptoms of anxiety so as to prevent panic and to keep anxiety at a facilitative level.

The third concept connected with Stage II is the notion that awareness of anxiety symptoms is to be used as a *signal to initiate coping responses*. This is a facilitative (see Chapter 6) interpretation of symptoms. The debilitative approach is to label the symptoms as dangerous or as signals to begin panicking. As you become a keen personal observer, you begin to spot signs of trouble and to take corrective action accordingly.

Stage III.   As a colleague of mine is wont to say: "Awareness and a quarter won't get you a cup of coffee." What he means is that by itself awareness is an empty entity that becomes powerful only when teamed up with action. What counts is what you do with the awareness. In our coping model the awareness is to lead to the application of one or more coping responses. Because it is the *action* following awareness that is important, I have urged you to familiarize yourself with, actively practice, and creatively design your twenty-one coping responses.

[2] Motofsky, D.I., and Balaschak, B.A. Psychological control of seizures. *Psychological Bulletin*, 1977, *84*, 723–750.

Anxiety is a tough nut: your anxious response to academics is probably an *overlearned,* almost automatic response. Therefore, it will take some powerful remedies and consistent effort to crack anxiety and "deautomatize" yourself. It's usually best to bring a coordinated combination of coping responses to bear against the symptoms of anxiety. Many of the twenty-one coping responses work nicely in tandem. A combination of them can be a stronger medicine than applying them singly or in piecemeal fashion. Our next section includes detailed examples that illustrate the use of multiple coping responses.

Again, the coping responses represent adaptive kinds of thoughts, behaviors, and attentional foci that are *incompatible* with your kinds of anxiety-producing, anxiety-exacerbating thoughts, behaviors, and attentional shifts.

Stage IV. During exams students may successfully use calming self-dialogue and rapid relaxation to reduce disturbingly high levels of anxious emotionality. But perhaps a few minutes later this emotionality reappears. This sort of situation calls for the reapplication of coping responses. However, for many students reapplication is the hardest stage to put into practice. They think that just because they took proper steps once, they've somehow immunized themselves against further anxiety attacks. In so many words these students are saying: "I've already calmed myself down once. Shouldn't that be enough?" Then a while later when anxiety symptoms reappear, as they predictably do, the students get discouraged, believe the coping responses don't work, and abandon the whole coping plan. They fail to realize that reapplication is the rule rather than the exception.

Anxiety control is not a one-time-only affair; rather, it is an ongoing process. You continually monitor yourself—

how are you feeling? what are you doing? where is your attention focused? what are you thinking about? what interpretations are you making of your academic situation?—and then choose and apply the appropriate coping responses.

Reapplication also involves some *experimentation*. For example, perhaps different combinations of coping responses will be more effective on second or third applications. Or perhaps rewording your anti-anxiety self-dialogue would prove more helpful.

What all this boils down to is that *consistent* reapplication of coping responses and *follow-through* are what really count. Concepts like "willpower" or "self-discipline" are unnecessary as long as you take proper and responsible action to cope with the indicators of anxiety.

Examples of the Model in Action

For each example, I present a hypothetical problem situation and suggest a coping response strategy using our anxiety control model. Although these are hypothetical examples, they represent composites of rather typical experiences of many academically anxious students. The purposes of the examples are to illustrate how the model works and how coping responses can be combined to form powerful anti-anxiety counterattacks. Remember, the examples are only guides, and I urge you to create your own versions of these coping responses and experiment with various combinations.

Example #1

Background information: Laurie is a second-term freshman nutrition major. She is the youngest of three children. Her father has been on disability retirement for two years following a heart attack. Her mother works as an accounting clerk. Because of the family circumstances, Laurie has felt additional pressure to make good. She has a partial scholarship, supplemented by family savings and income from her summer job. Laurie's plans are to earn registration as a dietician and to work eventually in a hospital or nursing-care facility.

The academic situation in question is an exam in a food science course. Laurie had studied conscientiously for the test and had gotten a proper amount of sleep the night before. She wanted to be at her sharpest since exam anxiety had been something of a problem for her. She tended to get edgy before exams and had experienced a little too much emotionality on some previous tests. She wanted to make an extra effort to be calm and prepared for this test.

On the day of the exam she walked into the classroom in a confident manner, pleased with how well she had kept her apprehension in check so far. However, the first part of the exam, consisting of several short-answer questions, proved disconcerting to her. The questions asked for the chemical compositions and actions of various food preservatives. This was material Laurie had reviewed, but her thoughts weren't focused, and she was recalling only fragments of information. At this point her poised manner began to unravel.

What Laurie became aware of: Fortunately, Laurie became quickly aware of early indicators of her emotional distress. For example, she became aware of . . .

> . . . an emerging feeling that, "if I could put words around it, would say: 'I know I can't do good now—I'm losing it.'"

. . . an element of panic and incoherence in her test-taking behavior—she was skipping around from item to item and frantically jotting down fragments of information that didn't hang together.

. . . jumbled thinking—her efforts at remembering facts were being blocked by worries and panicky self-talk.

. . . shifts in attention—she was aware of shifts in attention toward external distractors such as the exam room clock, the teacher, and her classmates.

What her awareness led to: Upon detecting these signs of anxiety, Laurie chose the following combination of responses:

Rapid Relaxation   Relaxing Imagery   Calming Self-Dialogue
(Coping Response +   (Coping Response +   (Coping Response
      #13)   #15)   #10)

                    Task-orienting Self-Directives
        +   (Coping Response #4)

Specifically, this is what Laurie did to cope:

Rapid Relaxation—Laurie progressed through the Rapid Relaxation procedures, using deep breathing to reduce her rising emotionality.

Relaxing Imagery—After performing Rapid Relaxation, Laurie followed with a personally relevant relaxing image. In her mind's eye, she envisioned how her father always soothingly reassured her. She could imagine him putting his arm around her and recall the feeling of caring that his fatherly touch communicated. She also heard his voice telling her: "You know your mother and I love you. You just relax and do what you can. We're always proud of you." Simple phrases, but for Laurie profoundly restorative ones, especially since in this imagery context she would accept their reassuring message.

Calming Self-Dialogue—After dwelling briefly on the preceding image, she reinforced her father's words with her own calming self-dialogue: "Come on, Laurie, let's pull you out of this tailspin. Remember, you did a pretty thorough review job. You came here with the facts in your head. You caught the panic just in time. Right now you're gaining on the problem, not 'losing it.' Okay . . . now relax and take another stab at those questions."

Task-Orienting Self-Directives—Now that she had succeeded in stemming her upward spiral of emotionality, Laurie emitted several Task-Orienting Self-Directives, self-commands to guide her test-taking behavior and to establish a creative "mind-set": "Focus on one item at a time. No need to jump around. Take the first one. Just let your mind go back to the page in the test where you read that information . . . [Pause] . . . Write down what you can recall . . . [Pause] Then put that information together into a clear answer."

Reapplication of coping responses. A few minutes later Laurie felt some twinges of panic reappear. She was working on another short-answer question, and when the solution was not immediately forthcoming she recognized an ominous feeling, like "the roof threatening to cave in on me." Laurie used her awareness of the reemergence of anxiety as a cue to reapply another combination of coping responses:

Self-Reminder (Coping Response + #12)	Calming Self-Dialogue (Coping Response #10) +	Refocusing Attention Back on Task (Coping Response #3)

Specifically, this is how Laurie reapplied coping responses:

Self-Reminder—Laurie performed a simple Self-Reminder
in order to put her worry into proper perspective:
"There you go again, feeling that the worst is going to
happen!"

Calming Self-Dialogue—She repeated her previous reassuring message to herself (see above).

Refocusing Attention—She instructed herself to calmly
turn her attention away from any worrisome ideation
and back to the test questions at hand.

Using our general coping model, we can diagram Laurie's
coping strategy:

Problems ⟶	Awareness ⟶	Coping Responses ⟶	Reapplication
1. Rising emotionality	Laurie became aware of the emergence of these problems and used their presence as a signal to employ coping responses	1. Rapid Relaxation +	When feelings of panic and disruptive mental activity reappeared, Laurie reapplied a combination of coping responses:
2. Panicky self-statements		2. Relaxing Imagery +	1. Self-Reminder +
3. Disorganized test-taking behavior		3. Calming Self-Dialogue +	2. Calming Self-Dialogue +
4. Attentional shifts onto external distractors		4. Task-Orienting Self-Directives	3. Refocusing Attention Back on Task

As we followed Laurie through the employment of the various stages of the coping model, several key ingredients stand out as part of her coping effort:

i. *She took time to reduce her high levels of emotionality.*

Instead of rushing ahead and letting anxiety snowball, Laurie resorted to relaxation. Her relaxation was timely, too, before panic got too far advanced. Of course, she had *practiced* the relaxation procedure so it was ready and available to her. Taking time out to calm oneself during an exam is time well spent. Too often students figure they haven't a moment to lose, and they fail to take the appropriate steps at the opportune time to manage their anxiety. On paper it appears that Laurie puts herself through a lengthy coping sequence, but actually these coping responses take only moments to carry out.

ii. *She identified the various elements of her upsetness.*

Laurie became aware of her rising emotionality, disorganized behavior, attentional shifts, and panicky thinking. She chose coping responses— relaxation, task-orienting self-directives, refocusing attention, and calming self-dialogue—that are incompatible with the aforementioned symptoms of anxiety.

iii. *She recognized the importance of keeping attention focused on task rather than on self-concerns.*

Her use of Refocusing Attention and Task-Orienting Self-Directives was designed to absorb herself in the test.

iv. *She interpreted her symptoms of anxiety as signals to cope, not as signals to disintegrate.*

This is the facilitative interpretation of anxiety symptoms that we discussed in Chapter 6.

Before moving on to Example #2, I have an issue for you to think through. Return to Laurie's "background information" section. What special meanings may Laurie have attached to her academic work so that it became more difficult or emotionally loaded? Would such meanings put Laurie at greater risk of interpreting her exams in ways that would lead to her symptoms of anxiety? If you were in her situation, how would *you* rethink those special meanings?

Example #2

Background information: Brad is a senior political science major. Despite high grades, he wonders what the future will bring. With the employment scene so tight, he believes his best plan is to continue his education, possibly in law school, in order to make himself more marketable. Brad's anxiety problem concerns the upcoming Law School Admissions Test (LSAT), which is only two days away. As the test date approaches, Brad has been having difficulty keeping in check worries and apprehension regarding the exam; in fact, he has gotten himself oversensitized to its importance.

What Brad became aware of: Now that the test is only two days off, Brad is becoming increasingly anxious. He's aware of several problems . . .

... worrisome ideation of the "What if . . . ?" variety—

"What if I get into the testing room and freeze?";
"What if I have a bad day? Everything depends on this one set of scores!"

... the emergence of a particularly frightening image—he imagines being mistakenly accused of cheating by the exam room proctor, when all he was doing was staring absentmindedly across the aisle at another student.

... whining and expressions of futility—"I never do well on these standardized exams. My scores won't reflect what I can really do!"

... feelings of almost electrifying terror immediately following his worries about the test.

What his awareness led to: Brad used his awareness of disturbing mental activity and emotionality as signals to begin coping. He chose the following coping response combination:

$$\underset{\text{(Coping Response \#3)}}{\text{Reanalyze "What if . . ."? Thinking}} + \underset{\text{(Coping Response \#14)}}{\text{Deep Muscle Relaxation}}$$

$$+ \underset{\text{(Coping Response \#18)}}{\text{Behavioral Rehearsal}}$$

Specifically, this is what Brad did to cope:

Reanalyze "What if . . . ?" Thinking—Brad paused in order to critically attack and think through the worries with which he was distressing himself. One worry that kept cropping up was: "What if I have a bad day?" He worried that he might not be at his mental or physical best on the day of the test. To counter this anxiety-engendering worry, Brad aggressively reanalyzed it from two points of attack. First, he thought through the presumed "usefulness" of this worry: "How am I helping myself by letting this worry run on and on in my head? Do I really think that worrying will make me any sharper come the day of the LSAT? Actually, if anything, my worrying has the effect of psyching me down!" Next, he reminded himself of some coping possibilities should even this worst fear materialize: "Okay . . . even if I have a bad day, I can turn around and take the LSAT the next time it's offered, in December. I'll have that second set of scores to mail off to law schools."

Deep Muscle Relaxation—The cumulative effect of his worrying had left Brad quite edgy and physically tense. After reanalyzing the main worry theme, he stretched out on his bunkbed and performed the abbreviated focusing/relaxing muscle relaxation exercise. He had already become proficient with the standard exercises in the tensing/relaxing routine. He spent several minutes focusing attention on the various muscle groups and achieving relaxation through suggestion. The most tightness was in his neck and shoulders, so he did some spot tensing and relaxing of those muscles to work out that tension.

Behavioral Rehearsal—While relaxed, Brad projected ahead to the day of the exam. He "ran a movie" through his mind of how the room, seating arrangements, and examinees might appear. He then directed attention on himself in the exam room. In his mind's eye, Brad rehearsed his test-taking behavior. He saw himself taking the test in a cool, efficient manner. He also imagined getting stuck on a question or two and then envisioned coping appropriately with those setbacks— working slowly rather than frantically, keeping a lid on maladaptive self-talk, and moving on to another test item if necessary. Brad used this coping response to reinforce his test-taking strategies and reconfirmed that he could stay on task and under control even if an unexpected setback were encountered.

Reapplication of coping responses. Brad realized that his worries about the LSAT could recur. When he became aware of their recurrence, he had at his disposal additional coping responses, which he used singly or in combination, to deal with the worries:

Reanalyze "What if" Thinking   OR   Thought-Stopping
(Coping Response #8)   (Coping Response #11)
OR   Hyperbolic Imagery
(Coping Response #2)

Specifically, this is how Brad *reapplied* coping responses:

Reanalyze "What if . . . ?" Thinking—When the worry resurfaced, Brad repeated his self-dialogue for refuting the "logic" behind the worry. Again, he used personally relevant, convincing language to pick apart and defuse the worry.

Thought-Stopping—On some occasions Brad might select thought-stopping as the coping response of choice in order to put the worry to rest. Remember, it is desirable to shut off or short-circuit the worry before it gets too entrenched. Brad's thought-stopping procedure consisted first of shouting the word "Stop" to himself and embellishing that command by imagining the sound of a loud whistle. This procedure interrupted the flow of the worry. He followed up the thought-stopping with a self-reminder that he was again disturbing himself with this worrisome mental activity and that he would be better served by directing attention elsewhere.

Hyperbolic Imagery—In order to drain away some of the distressing power of the worry, Brad developed a hyperbolic image that helped put the worry in an absurd perspective. He imagined he was breaking open the exam booklet. The first task was blackening the circles of the answer sheet where information like "name" and "social security number" was requested. However, Brad imagined that even this trivial task was too threatening. His hand began to tremble. Soon the trembling spread to his entire body. This shaking drew the attention of all in the room. The exam proctor tried in vain to calm him down. Presently a paramedic squad was summoned, and Brad saw himself being carried out of the room on a stretcher. The diagnosis? Terminal academic anxiety!

Using our general coping model, we can diagram Brad's coping strategy:

Problems ⟶	Awareness ⟶	Coping ⟶ Responses	Reapplication
1. Disruptive mental activity of the "What if . . . ?" variety	Brad became aware of the emergence of these problems and used their presence as a signal to begin coping	In order to quell his worries and panic, Brad chose a combination of coping responses: 1. Reanalyze "What if . . . ?" Thinking + 2. Deep Muscle Relaxation (using focusing/	As worries about the LSAT recurred during the evening, Brad reapplied several other coping responses to keep the worries in check: 1. Reanalyze "What if . . . ?" Thinking
2. Frightening mental images			
3. Expressions of whining and futility			
4. Subsequent feelings of terror and tension			

relaxing	OR
method)	2. Thought-
+	Stopping
3. Behavioral	OR
Rehearsal	3. Hyperbolic
	Imagery

As we followed Brad through the deployment of the various stages of the coping model, a couple of important ingredients stand out as part of his coping effort:

i. *He consistently attacks his worrisome ideation as it resurfaces.*

Brad utilized several coping responses that are incompatible with his stress-producing worries. Using his powers of critical thinking (reanalysis), thought-stopping, and hyperbolic imagery, Brad kept hammering away at the worry, slowly wearing down its ability to elicit anxious arousal. Fortunately, he accepted the fact that one application of a coping response is rarely sufficient to excise a pernicious worry.

ii. *He implemented behavioral rehearsal in order to practice coping adaptively with a potential problem situation.*

Brad used his powers of planful thinking to project ahead and rehearse his test-taking strategy. Behavioral rehearsal is a method for doing a "dry run" in one's mind of the actual event. Since Brad was concerned that during the exam he might disintegrate, he used mental imagery to reinforce desirable and adaptive test-taking behaviors. He even rehearsed how he could handle a frustration should one be encountered. But there's another angle here: Brad worried that he might not "feel" at his best on the exam day. Actually, it's not that he must *feel* his sharpest or most creative that is so important as it is what kind of overt and covert *behaviors* he engages in while taking the test. In other words, if he's careful to choose the right kind of behavior, his situation will take care of itself. As long as he's "acting" the role of the effective test-taker, he doesn't necessarily have to "feel" the part.

Example #3

Background information: Tracy is a sophomore communications arts major. She's not a serious student and readily admits that she's in college for social opportunities. Even so, she describes herself as a "hyper kind of person" who gets flustered across a broad range of evaluation situations. For example, she's very reluctant to speak in class for fear she might say something wrong and embarrass herself. She prefers to remain inconspicuous lest others see her presumed shortcomings and feel less positive toward her. The academic situation under consideration is her Comm. Arts test. She'd like to work on controlling academic anxiety so that she doesn't "fall to pieces" during tests. She feels it's ridiculous that she gets so worked up over an exam.

What Tracy became aware of: When the exam was distributed, Tracy became aware of a rapid onset of problems . . .

> . . . emotional and physiological distress—"My hands began sweating, and my stomach felt heavy, and

the more I thought about that the more frantic I felt!"

. . . negative and critical self-statements regarding her emotional and physiological distress—"This is so stupid! You shouldn't be so nervous! Quit acting like a jerk!"

. . . attention focused primarily on self-concerns instead of on the exam paper.

. . . The emergence of other disruptive mental activity, specifically panicky self-talk—"So I looked over the test when I got it, and I saw this question that asks you to list, define, and give examples of four types of nonverbal communication. This is a 30-point question! Well, I can only remember three, and one of those might be mixed up. So I'm thinking: 'You know, you just studied this *last night* and now you can't remember any of it! I mean, forgetting something in eight hours is senile! My God, am I losing my mind or something? I'll be lucky to get half of this right.' And then I really start freaking out."

What her awareness led to: Tracy used her awareness of disruptive mental activity and emotional distress as signals to begin coping. She chose the following coping combination:

Self-Reminder
(Coping Response #8) $+$ Refocusing Attention Back on Task
(Coping Response #3)

Specifically, this is what Tracy did to cope:

Self-Reminder—She paused briefly to remind herself that her overreaction to the question was uncalled for: "Just remember, you studied this stuff pretty thoroughly. You *are* prepared."

Refocusing Attention—Next, Tracy instructed herself to return her attention to the question and away from self-concerns.

Reapplication of coping responses. It turned out that Tracy's little coping combination (Self-Reminder and Refocusing Attention) *was not sufficient* to calm her down and improve her effectiveness. Those two coping responses were too weak to have much impact. Even after applying them, she still felt "strung out"; she was emitting more disruptive self-talk ("Oh God, I'm *still* tense!"), and her attention was still directed on self-concerns. Thus, *immediate* reapplication of coping responses—a different and more powerful combination—was called for.

Tracy used her awareness of these unabating symptoms of anxiety as a signal to reapply another combination of coping responses:

Calming Self-Dialogue   Rapid Relaxation   Acting Under Control
(Coping   +   (Coping   +   (Coping
Response #10)   Response #13)   Response #16)

+   Task-Orienting Self-Directives
(Coping Response #4)

Specifically, this is how Tracy *reapplied* these coping responses:

Calming Self-Dialogue—Tracy emitted some Calming Self-Dialogue to counter her panicky self-talk. Given her escalating state of emotional arousal, Tracy's best choice was a coping response that would undercut some of that anxiety. To herself she said: "Take it easy, Tracy—Let's get yourself pulled together—Just pause for a moment to calm down, that's the main thing—You can put this nervousness to rest—It's just a matter of selecting and practicing a few more coping responses."

Rapid Relaxation—Tracy progressed twice through the Rapid Relaxation procedures, using deep breathing to reduce her emotional arousal.

Acting under Control—Once she had achieved a calmer emotional state, Tracy aimed to modify her overt behavior toward the test. Acting Under Control helped her achieve a more confident, organized test-taking approach. In order to act the role of a supremely "in command" test-taker, she assumed a confident, squared posture; she took a slower, measured pace while answering the question; she eliminated her panicky internal dialogue; and she took a fresh piece of paper to use as a worksheet for developing an outline and tentative answer to the question.

Task-Orienting Self-Directives—With both emotionality and behavior under better control, Tracy turned to the next step: formulating an answer to the question regarding nonverbal communication. She engaged in a series of Task-Orienting Self-Directives in order to guide herself through an answer to the question: "Write down as much as you are sure about . . . Now let's see, one kind of nonverbal communication I definitely remember is called proxemics—how the distance between people communicates something about their relationship or culture . . . Write that down and give an example . . . Just write calm and smooth . . . Now think back to your notes and try to recall a second one . . . "

As anxious arousal, misdirected attention, inappropriate test-taking behaviors, and disruptive mental activity resurfaced during the exam, Tracy used various combinations of these and other coping responses to keep herself task-focused and to reduce escalating levels of emotionality.

Using our general coping model, we can diagram Tracy's coping strategy:

Problems ⟶ *Awareness* ⟶ *Coping Responses* ⟶ *Reapplication*

Problems	Awareness	Coping Responses	Reapplication
1. Emotional distress: feelings of franticness and physiological distress: sweating, stomach upset 2. Attention focused on self-concerns 3. Disruptive mental activity 　a. Negative and critical self-statements 　b. Panicky self-talk	Tracy became aware of the emergency of these problems and used their presence as a signal to employ coping responses . . .	1. Self-Reminder + 2. Refocusing Attention However, this combination was not effective for reducing her upsetness. Hence *immediate* reapplication of a stronger combination of coping responses was called for . . .	Since feelings of panic and disruptive mental activity persisted, Tracy reapplied a stronger combination of coping responses: 1. Calming Self-Dialogue + 2. Rapid Relaxation + 3. Acting Under Control + 4. Task-Orienting Self-Directives As she was aware of problems

resurfacing later during the exam, Tracy reapplied these and other combinations of coping responses

As we followed Tracy through the deployment of the various stages of the coping model, a couple of key ingredients stand out as part of her coping effort:

i. *She recognized that her first choice of coping responses was not effective.*

Sometimes a reapplication of coping responses without delay is needed. In Tracy's case, she benefited from an immediate reapplication of a different, more powerful coping response combination. Sometimes students think they can get by with just a "quick fix"—one or two weakly applied coping responses that they hope will be enough to allay their anxiety. Often this does not work. I recommend taking the time to implement a solid combination of coping responses.

ii. *When her initial coping effort proved ineffective, she refrained from making a negative interpretation.*

Tracy could have interpreted that event as a cue to get angry at the "failure" of the coping system or as a cue to worry even more about her "hopeless" state. Instead, the continuation of her upsetness was interpreted by Tracy as a time to bring different and more powerful efforts to bear against her anxiety.

Example #4

Background information: Phil is a junior chemistry major. He hopes to go on to graduate school and be involved in pharmaceutical research. Phil is the type of student whom friends characterize as "intense," "hard-working," and "serious." Indicative of this seriousness is Phil's hypervigilance to social and evaluative cues that might mean he's not "on top" of the situation or cues that might give him an edge on his competition. For example, he peeks to see what scores fellow classmates earned on tests, and he has a nose for what kind of classroom participation is most highly rewarded by his instructors.

Fortunately, he recognizes his tendencies to be too much on edge, to motivate himself through self-criticism, and to worry excessively. As a result, Phil engages in an ongoing process of monitoring what he tells himself about academics and checking his interpretations of evaluative situations. For example, he realizes that he resorts to worry to motivate himself for academic responsibilities. "If I'm worried about my work, I won't let myself get complacent" is the questionable logic he uses. However, he's already such a naturally serious student that it's superfluous to get more worked up by worrying. Phil bumps up against such anxiety-producing thinking time and again, but to his credit, he effortfully works at keeping it in check.

We encounter Phil as he is in the midst of a stressful academic preparation. He's attempting to write a program for his computer science course, but after more than one frustrating hour at his desk he has been unable to fathom the tricky programming language sequence. Now he's completely stuck, unsure how to proceed, and too naive about the language to diagnose the source of his stuckness.

What Phil became aware of: With progress at a standstill, Phil is becoming increasingly agitated. He's aware of several problems . . .

> . . . immobilization—no progress and little hope for any to be forthcoming.
> . . . "What if . . . ?" thinking—"What if I can't get this written on time? It's going to be murder trying to find terminal space!"
> . . . anger-engendering self-talk—"This screwy· professor doesn't explain anything clearly, and his crummy manual isn't any help either!"
> . . . "Why" questions—"Why do they let such an incompetent teach this course, anyway?"

What his awareness led to: Phil used his awareness of immobilization and disruptive mental activity as signals to begin coping. He chose the following coping response combination:

Countering Anger-Engendering
Self-talk
(Coping Respone #6)
+
Addressing "Why" Questions
(Coping Response #7)

+
Seeking Help
(Coping Response #17)

Specifically, this is what Phil did to cope:

Countering Anger-Engendering Self-Talk—Phil paused in order to straighten out the imbalanced thinking behind his anger and upsetness: "All right, granted the professor is no world-beater, and his manual has defects, too . . . But I certainly don't want to let my emotional life get bent way out of shape just because of his ineptness! Okay, so cool it . . . I'm only compounding the problem when I let this get under my skin."

Addressing "Why" Questions—Phil also reminded himself about the nonhelpful nature of the "Why" question that contributed to his feelings of bitterness and helplessness: "Why do they let this guy teach C. S. 301? Probably because nobody in the Comp. Sci. department knows just how bad he is. But that's beside the point . . . Later in the term when I fill out the course evaluation questionnaire, I'll write down some specific suggestions and criticisms to improve the course—Right now, I'll work on keeping myself under control and plugging along on the program."

Seeking Help—Given the impasse to progress, Phil decided that it would be most beneficial to seek out someone who could clearly explain to him the nuances of the computer language. Phil telephoned a friend, a computer science major who knew the subject and who could effectively impart his knowledge. Phil and his friend arranged an informal meeting for the next morning to discuss the program.

Reapplication of coping responses: After making the phone call, Phil put the program away and decided to spend the remaining study time finishing a lab report for his organic chemistry course. However, as he began the writeup, he noticed he was still thinking about and fretting over his computer assignment. As he became aware of the disruptive emergence of these concerns, he turned to a second combination of coping responses:

Stimulus Control of Worrying + Self-Reminder
(Coping Response #1)   (Coping Response #8)

Specifically, this is how Phil *reapplied* coping responses:

Stimulus Control—Phil set up a Stimulus Control procedure so that 50 minutes of his study hour would be spent efficiently writing the lab report. The remaining 10 minutes were reserved for uninterrupted fretting over the abandoned computer assignment. This worrying was to be performed as Phil sat on the edge of his bathtub.

Self-Reminder—If during the 50-minute work segment Phil became aware of an intrusive worry, he simply reminded himself of the Stimulus Control procedure and to turn attention back to the lab report.

Using our general coping model, we can diagram Phil's coping strategy:

Problems	→ *Awareness* →	*Coping Responses*	→ *Reapplication*
1. Immobilization 2. Disruptive mental activity a. "What if . . . ?" thinking b. Anger-engendering self-talk c. "Why" questions	Phil became aware of the emergence of these problems and used their presence as a signal to employ coping responses	1. Countering Anger-Engendering Self-Talk + 2. Addressing "Why" Questions + 3. Seeking Help	After moving on to work on a lab report, Phil was aware of the emergence of worries regarding his computer assignment. To cope with these intruding worries, he reapplied: 1. Stimulus Control of Worrying + 2. Self-Reminders

As we followed Phil through the deployment of the various stages of the coping model, several key ingredients stand out as part of his coping effort:

i. *He recognized that anxiety-management is an ongoing process.*

Whenever Phil is engaged in academic work, he is alert to the appearance of anxiety-producing thinking and maladaptive responses. He realizes that managing academic anxiety requires conscientious effort and the consistent application of restorative coping responses. As Phil implements the coping model, he becomes progressively more adept at achieving emotional balance.

ii. *After making the decision to postpone the computer assignment, he opted for a responsible alternative.*

After having experienced a setback with the computer program, Phil could easily have used that frustration as an excuse to abandon all study efforts for that evening. Instead, he chose a responsible alternative—using the remaining time to finish a lab report.

iii. *He construed the need for help in an appropriate light.*

Phil allowed himself to seek help without interpreting it as a sign of weakness, rude imposition, or indication of an intellectual shortcoming.

Example #5

Background information: Cindy is a junior studying mechanical engineering. At her university, she is one of only a handful of women in this curriculum. As a freshman, she had been apprehensive about enrolling in the engineering department. She feared nonacceptance by male students and faculty, and she feared that others would stereotype her as "unfeminine." Fortunately, her fears have not materialized. She has found substantial support from the department and fellow students. Moreover, Cindy is encouraged by the fact that more women are entering engineering and technical fields. She's excited that she is in the vanguard of this trend.

She is a more than adequate student, but she has not quite realized her potential. In fact, she could earn about half a letter grade more if she put in better test-taking performances. Commonly, she finds on returned exams that she lost points because she missed some given information or made some trivial computational error. Cindy's test-taking problem is due to *reduced cue utilization* (see Chapter 4). These errors result because her attention is being somehow fragmented or diverted from the test so that she fails to fully apprehend the essential information. Additionally, Cindy may be rushing herself so that careless mistakes are more likely to occur.

The evaluative situation under consideration is an exam in one of Cindy's engineering courses, fluid mechanics. Questions that concern us are: how does her reduced cue utilization problem result? how does her test-taking behavior break down? how does she rectify the problem of reduced cue utilization?

What Cindy became aware of: Cindy perused the first set of exam questions. They looked somewhat similar to some she had solved for homework, but the relationship was not immediately apparent. As she began the problems, she became aware of . . .

. . . a persistent type of absolutistic thinking—"You *should* know right away what they're asking for."

. . . an erroneous "If . . . then" conclusion—"If you're planning to be any kind of an engineer, then you're supposed to be able to zero right in on the answer."*

. . . panicky behavior—she was starting to push herself to put numbers and equations on paper.

. . . attention misdirected to external distractors—she glanced again and again at the exam room clock.

. . . physiological indicators of anxiety—muscle tightness and sweating hands.

. . . emotional indicators of anxiety—a swelling of panic or "clutching."

What her awareness led to: Upon detecting these signs of anxiety, Cindy chose the following combination of coping responses:

Attacking Absolutistic Thinking 　　　Rapid Relaxation
(Coping Response #19)　　+　(Coping Response #13)

Task-Orienting Self-Directives
(Coping Response #4)

Specifically, this is what Cindy did to cope:

Attacking Absolutistic Thinking—Cindy paused in order

---

* Take a close look at the two kinds of self-talk that Cindy is engaging in at this moment. Note that she uses absolutistic thinking and erroneous conclusions as "operating principles" to regulate her test-taking behavior. As a result, she is expecting herself to come up with almost instantaneous correct solutions to the test questions. Such internal dialogue *increases* the level of evaluative stress. Hence, Cindy will cause herself to experience more anxiety. Of course, one of the results of increased anxiety is poorer functioning of one's attentional processes.

to debunk the specious absolutistic thinking that was fomenting unnecessary evaluative stress: "Hey, wait a minute. Who says I'm supposed to be able to instantaneously achieve the right answer or have perfect insight into an engineering problem? I mean, who am I, Einstein? I *can* take time to think through a problem, and that doesn't mean I'm any less gifted than my peers."

Rapid Relaxation—After putting her erroneous thinking into perspective, Cindy took herself through the Rapid Relaxation procedure to reduce her subjective state of disturbing emotionality. (Of course, she had already become proficient with Rapid Relaxation so as to have this technique available for just such an occasion).

Task-orienting Self-directives—Cindy emitted a series of TOSD's to keep her attention squarely on task, to apprehend all the information embedded in the test question, to work at an appropriate pace, and to guide herself through the various calculations needed to solve the problem. Cindy's TOSD's appear as follows: "Read the question all the way through a couple of times . . . What are they asking for? They want me to determine the direction of flow through a circular tube and the quantity of flow in liters per second . . . Okay . . . I'll use the Hagen-Poiseuille equation for this . . . Write it down . . . Now write down the given information . . . Work out each term of the equation separately, because there's no need to rush . . . Take your time to recheck those figures . . . Okay . . . Now first find the average velocity, V, in meters per second . . . Divide that ratio, and watch the decimal point . . . "

Reapplication of coping responses: As Cindy worked her way through the question, she could feel an urge to rush herself along, and she noticed a split in attention from her test page to the exam room clock. Also, she could sense that her irrational "need" for quick closure to the question was resurfacing. At this point Cindy used her awareness of the reemergence of these signals as a cue to reapply a combination of coping responses:

$$\text{Self-Reminder} \atop \text{(Coping Response \#12)} \quad + \quad {\text{Acting Under Control} \atop \text{(Coping Response \#16)}}$$

Specifically, this is how Cindy *reapplied* coping responses:

Self-Reminder—Cindy acknowledged that she was slipping back into trouble, and she used the Self-Reminder as a simple self-corrective device: "You're pushing yourself again. Remember, there's no need to come up with immediate answers. Keep in mind that success in engineering results more from hard work and trial and error than from instant insight."

Acting Under Control—After the reminder to lift the pressure on herself, Cindy chose an interesting and creative variant to the Acting Under Control coping responses: Cindy has been a tutor for a female freshman engineering student. She helps this student with her homework sets and explains lecture material to her. Now on the exam, Cindy pretended that she was solving this test question as though she were acting as a tutor for an imaginary student. By acting the part of the tutor, Cindy would be required to assume an authoritative approach, look and sound in command, explain the rationale for deriving various equations, and proceed in a slow and clear manner to make sure the "student" understood each step. Thus, Cindy talked herself through the solution of the test question all the while pretending she was authoritatively and lucidly tutoring an imaginary student. Cindy's Acting Under Control coping response was a highly creative method for ensuring attentiveness to task and to task-relevant information.

Using our general coping model, we can diagram Cindy's coping strategy:

Problems ⟶	Awareness ⟶	Coping Responses ⟶	Reapplication
1. Absolutistic thinking	Cindy became quickly aware of the emergence of these problems and used their presence as a signal to employ coping responses	1. Attacking Absolutistic Thinking + 2. Rapid Relaxation + 3. Task-Orienting Self-Directives	A few minutes later, Cindy became aware of her fragmenting attentional focus and "need" to push for quick closure to the test question. She reapplied a different combination of coping responses in order to regain a sense of control: Self-Reminder + Acting Under Control (imaginary tutoring session)
2. Erroneous "If . . . then" conclusion			
3. Panicky behavior			
4. Attention misdirected to external distractors			
5. Physiological and emotional distress			

As we followed Cindy through the deployment of the various stages of the coping model, a key ingredient stands out as part of her coping effort:

i. *She "tuned in" to the patterns of disruptive mental activity (absolutistic thinking and erroneous "If . . . then" conclusion) that contributed to excessive evaluative stress.*

   We saw that Cindy harbored the dubious notion that if she were a "good" or adequate engineering student, she should be able to focus right in on the solutions to test questions. Unfortunately, this kind of thinking mediates maladaptive test-taking behaviors: Cindy could rush herself along too quickly and in the process disregard essential information. To her credit, Cindy was able to "hear" the demands she was making of herself and to confront them with sensible counterarguments. By attacking her absolutistic thinking and erroneous assumptions, she was able to reduce the pressure she was exerting on herself and hence able to take a more controlled approach to the test question.

HOMEWORK

I hope the five examples adequately familiarized you with how the model works. Now I urge you to perform these homework exercises, since they will help you become adept at using the model.

Exercise 1.   Take a piece of paper and divide it into two columns. Next, think back to a recent exam or academic situation in which you experienced anxiety. Try to recall as many particulars of that academic situation as you can. In the left column *write down in detail (specify)* the problems you encountered or the symptoms of anxiety that were present. In the right column *write down in detail (specify)* an effective combination of coping responses that, in retrospect, you might have applied at that time to reduce anxiety and improve your task effectiveness. Put on your thinking cap to fashion creative, powerful coping responses. A two-column example could look like this:

Problems Encountered/ Symptoms of Anxiety	*Coping Combinations*
I. Walking across quad to test Aware of: a. Frightening image of failure (give description of image) b. Stomach upset	I. Coping Responses Employed: a. Calming Self-Dialogue (write out dialogue word-for-word) b. Rapid Relaxation c. Competency Imagery (give detailed description of image)
II. Got to exam room and saw others doing last-minute cramming Aware of: a. Panicky thinking (include word-for-word description) b. Negative and critical self-statement (include word-for-word) c. Attention directed to other classmates	II. Coping Responses Employed: a. Calming Self-Dialogue (write out dialogue word-for-word) b. Disputed negative self-statement (include verbal disputation) c. Focused attention elsewhere

Exercise 2. Now comfortably recline on your bed or in an overstuffed chair. This exercise uses your powers of

imagining to cope with the problems and symptoms you just described. For the sake of clarity, I'll use the information from the Exercise 1 example above. Vividly picture in your mind's eye the first problem on the list. In this case, it's walking across the quad to the exam. Call to mind the actual thoughts or frightening imagery that were in your consciousness at that time. Revivify the physiological distress. As you recall this experience in the here-and-now, let yourself get just a bit anxious. After perhaps a minute, cut that scene short and envision yourself coping with these symptoms of anxiety from the list. To yourself, engage in a Calming Self-Dialogue using the personally relevant and convincing language from the right-hand column. Actually practice a series or two of Rapid Relaxation as you are reclined. Call forth a clear, effective Competency Image. See if this coping combination helped quell the twinge of anxiety you had just felt. For each problem situation on your list, practice its accompanying coping combination. You may want to revise the combination if it doesn't feel effective. To sum up, the steps for Exercise 2 are as follows:

   i. Get in a comfortable reclined position.
  ii. Call to mind the first problem situation from your list. Picture this situation as vividly as possible. Recall the actual thoughts and feelings experienced at that time.
 iii. As you recollect that incident, you may feel a small amount of anxiety. That's okay, but cut the scene short before the anxiety becomes uncomfortable.
 iv. In your mind's eye, see yourself employing an effective combination of coping responses that would prove incompatible with the symptoms of

anxiety. Carry through with each coping response from your list. For example, repeat to yourself the actual words or phrases in your restorative internal dialogue.

v. Experiment to see if these coping responses actually reduced the state of anxiety that was elicited earlier in the exercise.

Exercise 3. Exercises 1 and 2 were based on *past* academic situations. In Exercise 3, project ahead to a *future* evaluative situation like a quiz or test. As before, divide a piece of paper into two columns. In the left column *write down in detail* (specify) the problems— worries, negative interpretations, misdirected attention, immobilization, disruptive emotionality—that you *anticipate* or *predict* are likely to occur on this upcoming evaluative event. In the right column *write down in detail* (specify) effective coping response combinations for each.

Exercise 4. Again, seek out a comfortable surface on which to recline. Like Exercise 2, Exercise 4 involves the use of mental imagery. But this time you are to call to mind the *anticipated* problem or symptom from Exercise 3. For a minute or less, dwell on this anticipated problem situation. If a distressing level of anxiety is experienced at any time, cut the image short. Next, see yourself applying the written coping responses from Exercise 3 that are incompatible with anxiety. Exercise 4 is a kind of behavioral rehearsal: specific potential problem situations are imagined, and potential methods for coping with them are imagined as well. If practiced properly, Exercise 4 can help you prepare for anxiety-arousing situations.

Summary

Previous chapters familiarized you with the various characteristics or symptoms displayed by academically anxious students. We also developed twenty-one coping responses that prove incompatible with anxiety.

In this chapter I introduced you to a four-stage general coping model whereby various coping responses can be combined into powerful countermeasures against the symptoms of anxiety.

Stage One represents the emergence of the various symptoms common to academic anxiety. Stage Two of the model emphasizes early detection (awareness) of the emergence of the symptoms; they are much easier to deal with if arrested early. Stage Three involves the implementation of a coordinated combination of coping responses that are incompatible with an anxious state. Finally, Stage Four encourages reapplication of the same or different coping responses when symptoms reappear.

Five detailed examples were provided that illustrated the use of the model in action. Following the examples, four homework exercises were suggested that provide the reader practice in applying the model.

Suggested Reading

*Barrow, John. Cognitive self-control strategies with the anxious student. *Psychotherapy: Theory, Research and Practice*, 1979, *16*, 152–157.

Beery, R. G. Fear of failure in the student experience. *Personnel and Guidance Journal*, 1975, *54*, 190–203.

Haburton, Eleanor. Study skills for college. Cambridge, Mass.: Winthrop Publishers, 1981. (Especially Part V, Controlling Test-Taking Anxiety).

* Directed primarily at a professional audience but still worth a look.

Millman, Jason, and Pauk, Walter. *How to take tests*. New York: McGraw-Hill Paperback, 1969. (Tips and techniques for improving test-taking skills)

Pauk, Walter. *How to study in college*. Boston: Houghton Mifflin Co., 1974. (second edition)

*Sarason, Irwin G. (ed.) *Test anxiety: Theory, research, and applications*. Hillsdale, N.J.: Lawrence Erlbaum Associates, 1980.

*Wine, Jeri. Test anxiety and direction of attention. *Psychological Bulletin*, 1971, 76, 92–104.

Woolfolk, Robert L., and Richardson, Frank C. *Stress, sanity, and survival*. New York: Signet, 1978. (Especially pp. 38–50).

CHAPTER 9

Developing
Test-Taking Skills

The preceding chapters have dealt with managing academic anxiety by rethinking the meanings attached to academics, redirecting attentional focus, engaging in task-oriented self-directives, practicing rapid relaxation, and so forth. In Chapter 8 we presented a model for coordinating selected Coping Responses into an anxiety management system. In this concluding chapter we shall discuss some practical but effective exam preparation methods and test-taking strategies.

Being well prepared for an exam is fundamental to reducing academic anxiety. Obviously, students who have mastered the subject matter and are able to demonstrate that mastery on an exam are likely to possess greater self-confidence. That self-confidence translates itself into more task-focused attention, less anxiety-engendering self-talk, and less avoidant behavior.

The topics covered in this chapter should help you become a better-prepared test-taker. Specifically, we shall cover four topic areas: (1) developing an environment conducive to studying and concentration; (2) suggestions for effective preexamination preparation; (3) confidence-building strategies for exam day; and (4) tips for taking objective and essay exams.

The Proper Study Environment

Getting yourself prepared for an exam depends upon your having a distraction-free study environment. The proper environment is probably not your residence-hall room. Through trial and error many students find a study niche that affords few interruptions, low background noise, and comfortable heat and light. That niche may be a study-mate's apartment, a library carrel, a designated study lounge, or an unoccupied classroom.

No matter where they are located, all good study environments have one thing in common: a minimum of distractions. Distractions impede learning. Obviously, the most efficient studying will occur in an environment where you can focus as much attention as possible on your study materials.

Which of your study locations provides the best environment? A Study Distractions Analysis Scale[1] used at St. John's University Counseling Center can help you make that evaluation. Take a few moments to respond to this scale:

List three places where you study in the order you most use them:

A _____ B _____ C _____

Now check the column that applies to each of those places. (T = True, F = False)

[1] Price, G.E., & Griggs, S.A. *Counseling college students through their learning styles.* ERIC/CAPS Publication, 1985, pp. 56–57.

	Place A		Place B		Place C	
1. Other people often interrupt me when I study here.	T	F	T	F	T	F
2. Much of what I can see here reminds me of things that have nothing to do with studying.	T	F	T	F	T	F
3. I often hear radio or TV when I study here.	T	F	T	F	T	F
4. I often hear the phone ringing when I study here.	T	F	T	F	T	F
5. I think I take too many breaks when I study here.	T	F	T	F	T	F
6. I seem to be especially bothered by distractions here.	T	F	T	F	T	F
7. I usually don't study here at a regular time each week.	T	F	T	F	T	F
8. My breaks tend to be too long when I study here.	T	F	T	F	T	F
9. I tend to start conversations when I study here.	T	F	T	F	T	F
10. I spend time on the phone here that I should use for study.	T	F	T	F	T	F

11. There are many things here that have nothing to do with study or schoolwork. T F T F T F

12. Temperature conditions here are not very good for studying. T F T F T F

13. Chairs, table, and lighting arrangements here are not very helpful for studying. T F T F T F

14. When I study here, I often am distracted by certain individuals. T F T F T F

15. Here I have a place that I can use for study and nothing but study. T F T F T F

Total the checks in each column. The column with the most "true" checks may be the poorest place to study.

Finding a relatively distraction-free study environment is your first objective. Next you can select study *methods* that "pull for" concentration.

What I *don't* recommend is the familiar "fetal" study position: student curled up in a chair with book propped on knees. This passive posture (often accompanied by indiscriminate underlining of text) does not result in sharp concentration. Try changing to an *active* study approach that demands a concentrative effort. For example, instead of passively rereading the material, make up quiz questions

234 ◇ COPING WITH ACADEMIC ANXIETY

to ask yourself about it. Or pretend you are lecturing the material to a class. Or imagine you are explaining the concepts during a tutoring session. Similarly, if your study material consists of problems or equations to solve, find an unused classroom and work out the problems on the blackboard as if you were presenting them for a class. Such active study methods whereby you "attack" the material allow for more focused concentration.

How does one properly prepare for an exam? Following are some ideas for performing effective review and getting mentally and physically prepared.

The What, How, and When of Review

1. Note that I don't use the phrase, "study for a test." *"Review for a test"* is the correct term. Reviewing means that original learning has already taken place. If you are studying the material for the first time in preparation for an exam, you place yourself in double jeopardy: You probably won't have time to absorb the material, and that can result in your feeling anxious at exam time.

   The purpose of review is to consolidate what you have learned and to combat forgetting. Your study and review for each test should have started from the first day of class as you continually read and reviewed your test, classnotes, and textnotes. That is part of the "when" of review.

2. Make sure you attend class the day before the exam. Be certain of the *structure* of the exam: objective or essay? or a combination of the two? how many questions? how will points be distributed across the questions? will material from the test or lectures be stressed?

3. During your previous studying and class attendance you should have made note of:
   - Key terminology, formulas, definitions;
   - Items in lists (*e.g.*, the main reasons for the War of 1812; characteristics of an ecosystem; children's developmental milestones);
   - Points emphasized in class.
4. Certainly you will review your text and notes, but also consult other sources for review: friends' classnotes, previous tests or quizzes (these may be found in someone's previous semester file), and review questions at the end of text chapters. You might also consult the library for other textbooks that present the same material from a somewhat different perspective. Perhaps another introductory biology, psychology, or accounting text explains a concept more clearly than does the book your class is using.
5. Use a variety of review methods:
   - Make up 3″ × 5″ flash cards containing key vocabulary, ideas, definitions. These cards can be used for self-testing.
   - Ask for help *ahead of time* if you need it. Question the instructor or teaching assistant or friends if you need clarification. As we recall from Coping Response #17 in Chapter 7 (Seeking Help), don't talk yourself out of getting help if you need it.
   - Form review groups with a few friends and practice teaching or quizzing each other.
   - Recite the information to yourself. Do this recitation *out loud*; that will help in committing the material to memory.
6. Review for an upcoming midterm exam should

begin three to five days ahead of time. Have a specific plan and time schedule for review. By all means use a written schedule log to keep track of your review plans. Use a schedule log like the one below:

Date	Review Plan	Time Allotted	What I Actually Accomplished
10/10	Prepare flash cards (at least 24) for formula and definition review.	45 min.	Spent 1 hr making 27 flash cards.
10/11	Review chaps 5, 6, and 8. Pay attention to highlighted text. Review textbook notes.	2 hrs	Accomplished all in 1½ hrs!
10/12	Meet with study group to quiz each other on selected problems from notes and chapter study questions.	1.5 hrs.	Met with group for 2 hrs total.
10/13	Review lecture notes and flash cards. Commit formulas to memory.	1 hour	Done! Ready for tomorrow.
10/14	EXAM DAY		

Mental and Physical Preparation

While you are reviewing for a test, try not to change your normal routine. Get enough sleep, don't skip meals, and make sure that you engage in some quality recreation activities. By all means, build in some study break time during your review.

Know how to budget your time during an exam. It's a

good idea to have a *game plan* for allocating your time during the exam. For example, assume you are preparing for a one-hour exam. How many minutes should you allow for each of the following:

a. Skimming the test to acquaint yourself with the types of questions and to identify those questions to answer first _____ minutes.
b. 25 objective (T/F and multiple-choice) items worth one point each _____ minutes.
c. 5 short answer questions worth 5 points each (25 points total) _____ minutes.
d. 1 essay question worth 25 points _____ minutes.
e. Checking answers _____ minutes.

Allocate three or four minutes for skimming and five minutes for checking answers. Since the three sections contain equivalent point totals, plan on spending equal time on each—in this case, 17 minutes apiece after allowing for skimming and checking.

Do any final reviewing on the evening before the exam. Make this review the *last* reading or studying that you perform that night. Go right to bed after the review. Do not watch a TV show or read a magazine, as that will interfere with the learning that you just laid down in your mind. While you sleep, your mind can unconsciously consolidate that material you reviewed.

Finally, go to bed early enough to ensure a decent night's sleep. Avoid caffeinated beverages, which will interfere with sleep and make you feel jittery.

Boosting Confidence on Exam Day

Chapter 8 introduced you to a four-stage coping model. You employ this model whenever you become aware of the emergence of anxiety symptoms—misdirected attention, interfering thoughts, emotional distress, or inappropriate behavior. This section introduces you to ten *primary prevention* tips for exam day. I call them that because you can use them even when anxiety symptoms are not evident. Put the tips into practice to *prevent* anxious arousal.

1. If the exam is in the morning, allow enough time to shower, freshen up, and breakfast. Eat a moderate breakfast to tide yourself over the exam. A doughnut or sweet roll is not adequate. Supplement those carbohydrates with protein such as in milk, cottage cheese, or an egg or two. Go easy on caffeinated beverages.

2. Practice cultivating a positive attitude about the exam. Be on guard against disruptive self-talk. Review Chapter 5 for examples of that. Through what kind of lens are you viewing this exam? As a threat to self-esteem, or as an opportunity to demonstrate what you know? As a challenge to be relished, or as a pain to be endured?

3. Have all of your test-taking materials ready to go—pens, pencils, calculator (and spare battery), scratch paper, watch, textbook and notes if "open book" exam, etc. Don't wait until the last moment to pull these materials together.

4. Get to the exam room with time to spare. Lateness will generate a host of anxiety-engendering thoughts that can be difficult to quell.

5. Avoid "anxiety-generating" students—those doing feverish last-minute cramming or catastrophizing.

6. You may prefer to sit in a sparsely occupied section of the room. Also, you may want to use the few minutes before the exam to review your notes and/or flash cards or to recall certain formulas or equations. Focus your attention on this mental activity instead of on distressing personal thoughts.

7. Don't plunge into the exam without making sure you understand all the directions and what kind of responses the instructor is expecting. This tip may seem ludicrously obvious, but as a teacher and counselor I've seen quite a few students lose points and fret needlessly because they were not sure what was expected. On a recent exam the instructor required only that the students *set up* the equations for solving a problem. Sure enough, two students lost time and points struggling to solve the equations after setting them up.

8. If you memorized key formulas, equations, or vocabulary and you are concerned that you will forget them, as soon as you are handed the exam write out those items on the back of the exam or on scratch paper.

9. Have at your disposal several methods that can bring about a quick reduction in tension. Take some favorite candy along (mints, lozenges, or bite-size licorice) to pop into your mouth. Be ready to practice Rapid Relaxation (Coping Response #13). An effective "time out" from the tension of an exam is a request to leave the room for a drink of water.

10. During the test, by all means ask the instructor for clarification if you don't understand a question

or are not sure you are answering the question as intended. Instructors are usually receptive to requests for clarification, and quite often they let slip a hint or two about how to answer the question.

Exam-Taking Tips

Objective test items require the ability to recall or recognize facts, ideas, and/or relationships. Objective tests usually consist of true-false, multiple choice, and matching or completion questions. Following are some specific tips for answering those types of questions.

Objective Questions: General Tips

1. Make sure you know whether there is a penalty for guessing. If there is no penalty, it is certainly in your favor to guess.
2. Read the directions twice, and underline all key words.
3. Plan your time. Survey the exam and set up a time budget.
4. Always begin by answering those questions you are sure about. That helps build confidence and accrues points.
5. Don't read too much into the questions. Assume that they have straightforward rather than trick answers.
6. Don't spend too much time mulling over answers. The most obvious answer is usually the correct one.
7. Pay attention to items that bear some similarity. You may be able to learn enough from ques-

tions early in the test to help you answer later questions.

8. If you are using a separate answer sheet, be certain that the test item you are working on corresponds with the item number on your answer sheet.

9. Place check marks next to those items you don't answer. Come back to them after you have answered all that you know.

10. When you check your answers, if you come across what appears to be a wrong answer, by all means change it. Do so even though it goes against conventional wisdom that says your first response is always the correct one.

True-False Questions: Specific Tips

1. True-false questions that contain qualifiers such as "probably," "generally," "sometimes," "usually," and so forth *tend* to be true.

2. Questions with absolute words like "never," "always," "none," and so forth *tend* to be false.

3. Some true-false questions consist of two independent clauses. If one of these clauses contains a false statement, then the entire question must be marked false.

4. If a question is partly true and partly false, mark it false. For example: "Chicago, a large Midwestern city on the shore of Lake Michigan, is the capital of Illinois." Much of the sentence is true, but part of it is false. Hence, the whole item must be marked false.

5. With true-false questions, the instructor is probably seeking to determine whether you know when

and under what circumstances something is true or not.

Multiple-Choice Questions: Specific Tips

1. If one choice is significantly longer (or shorter) than the others, it is usually the correct choice.

2. The most complete and inclusive answer is frequently the correct one. (That tends to make it the longest, or wordiest, choice).

3. Remember that sometimes all choices may be partially correct. You must then choose the *best* choice.

4. Read all the possible choices to the question rather than just seeking out the correct choice.

5. Cross out obviously wrong choices and concentrate on those remaining.

6. "None of the above" is usually a wrong choice.

7. When the question stem and alternatives do not make grammatical sense, the alternatives are wrong. For example: The _____ maintain calcium and phosphorous metabolism. (A) thymus (B) thyroid gland (C) parathyroids (D) pituitary.

   The correct answer must be (C) because the verb in the stem requires a plural noun.

8. If two alternatives are the same except for one word, one of those alternatives is usually the correct one.

9. If you are certain that two alternatives are correct *and* another alternative is "all of the above," then "all of the above" should be the correct choice.

10. Alternatives that contain absolute qualifiers (*e.g.*, "never", "always") tend to be wrong.

11. One of the middle alternatives (*e.g.*, choice B or

choice C), especially one with the most words, is often the correct choice.
12. A choice is likely to be wrong if it contains terminology unknown to you or it is silly or humorous.

Matching Questions: Specific Tips

1. Read both columns to be matched. Do this to get an understanding of the alternatives, because frequently there will be two or three extra, unmatchable items in one column.
2. Start with those items you are sure of. Cross off the items as you match them so that you systematically shorten the list.
3. After you have matched all items you are sure of, you are down to a process of elimination. If guessing is not penalized, make your best guess as to the remaining match-ups.

Completion Questions: Specific Tips

With completion questions, the instructor has left blank a key element. Usually a word or short phrase is missing, and you must fill in the blank with the missing element.

1. Watch for grammatical clues that might put you on the right track: To a _____, the glass is always half empty; to an _____, the glass is always half full. (If you couldn't remember the distinction between optimist and pessimist, the grammatical structure should give you a clue.)
2. If you cannot recall the exact word, go ahead and write down a phrase or sentence fragment that

would be equivalent to that word. You may receive partial credit.

3. The number of blank spaces provided can give you a clue to the right answer. Example: "_____ _____" was Sinclair Lewis's first acclaimed novel. (If you weren't sure whether the answer was *Main Street* or *Babbitt*, you may be able to answer with more confidence.)

Essay Questions

Essay questions test your ability to *express yourself* expositively; to *interpret* subject matter; and to *organize* material into a coherent answer. Your answer to an essay question should demonstrate that:

1. You understand what is being asked;
2. You know the subject matter;
3. You can produce an answer that is organized and coherent.

Before we discuss the specifics of taking essay exams, let's review some general strategies:

1. Carefully read all the essay questions before you decide on answering one. Frequently instructors give you a choice of essay questions. Choose those that you feel most confident about.
2. After you have chosen questions to answer, take a few minutes to jot down on scratch paper or the back of the exam paper any key facts or information you have memorized that you will want to refer back to.

3. To answer an essay question, you must understand precisely what is being asked. In my experience as a teacher, I find that many students lose points because they answer questions tangentially or fail to address the issue being asked. Pay close attention to any *directional words* such as compare, evaluate, explain. We shall come back to this point later.

4. Make a brief outline of your answer before you plunge into the writing. Spend some time organizing and structuring your answer. Know what you want to say and the argument you plan to make *before* you write.

5. After making the outline, budget your time. Note how many minutes you will spend on each question, and stick to that budget.

6. Depending on the type of question asked, plan to answer the question in the first paragraph. The first paragraph is where you make the essential comparisons, argument, contrast, or evaluation. Use the following paragraphs to clarify your answer and supply information or evidence to buttress your points. Your last paragraph should be a summary of your argument.

7. Finally, take time at the end to reread your answer—check for grammar glitches, punctuation, spelling, and readability. Also read it through to "hear" how it sounds—does it make sense? does it say what you wanted to say?

Let's return to a point made in item 3 above—that to answer an essay question you must understand what is being asked. Your essay questions will contain a key word—a *directional* word that will tell you how your instructor wants you to respond to the question and how your answer should be structured. Many students lose points unnecessarily because their answers do not correspond with the directions. Other students would find much of their anxiety allayed if they focused on the specific task asked of them.

Below are some directional words that appear again and again in essay questions. Familiarize yourself with their meanings so that your essay answer will properly correspond to what is being asked.

Analyze: Provide the nature of the parts and the relationship of the parts to each other and to the whole.

Compare: Examine qualities or characteristics to discover resemblances. Frequently one is asked to "compare with," which implies that one is to emphasize similarities, although some differences may be mentioned.

Contrast: Stress the dissimilarities, differences, or unlikeness of associated things, ideas, events, or problems.

Criticize: Express your judgment with respect to the correctness or merit of the factors under consideration. Give the results of your own analysis and discuss the limitations and good points or contribution of the plan or work in question.

Define: Give a concise, clear, and authoritative meaning. Details are not required, but briefly draw boundaries or limitations around the definition. Keep in mind what differentiates the particular object from others.

Describe: Recount, characterize, sketch, or relate in narrative form the chief characteristics of a situation or retell the essential features of a story.

Discuss: Examine, analyze, and present considerations for or against the problem or issue involved. Give a complete and detailed answer.

Evaluate: Present a careful appraisal of the problem, topic, or issue. Stress advantages and disadvantages.

Explain: Give reasons for what is being asked. Clarify and interpret the material. State the "how" and the "why." Account for any different opinions or contradictory results. State what are considered to be the causes of the event(s) in question.

Interpret: Translate, solve, or comment upon the subject and give your own judgment or reaction to the issue.

List: Present an itemized series. Be concise.

Outline: Provide an organized description. Give the main points and essential supplementary information. Omit minor details. Present the information in a systematic arrangement or classification scheme.

Prove: Evaluate and cite evidence. Where needed, provide logical or mathematical proof. Provide confirmation or verification of a point.

Review: Provide a critical examination and sum-
                mary. Analyze and comment briefly, in
                an organized sequence, upon the major
                points of the problem.

State: Express the main points in brief, clear,
                narrative form. Details and examples
                may be omitted. This term is similar to
                specify, *give*, or *present*.

Summarize: Give a description or historical sequence
                or development from the point of origin
                of some event.

Essay Questions: Specific Tips

If running out of time during an essay exam or budgeting
time ineffectively is your problem, you might try:

- Dividing up the total time you have to answer a
  question based upon several criteria: (1) total time
  you have for the test; (2) how many questions need
  to be answered; (3) point value of the questions; and
  (4) questions that can be answered most quickly.
- Jotting down the time you allow for each essay
  alongside the question.
- Making a concerted effort to stick to the time you
  have allotted.
- Outlining answers if you don't have time to write a
  complete answer.

If your problem is not knowing what is being asked for in
a question, you might try:

- Reacquainting yourself with the directional words
  above.

- Studying how the question is written to get clues as to how to organize an answer.
- Ask the instructor for clarification.

If your problem is producing disorganized answers, you might try:

- Jotting down, before you tackle the question, key words, details and examples, main ideas, brief outline of the introduction, body of the answer, and summary paragraph.
- Making your introductory statement or paragraph a summary of your answer.
- Proofreading your answer for content, organization, and grammar.

If your problem is excess wordiness, you might try:

- Saying what you mean in standard, conversational English.
- Using an outline to guide your writing so that it forces you to be economical.
- Knowing the difference between padding your answer and elaborating on key points.
- Stating the main ideas and giving examples, facts, or details to support them.

If your problem is simply not knowing an answer, you might try:

- Moving on to a question you can answer so as to maximize your point total on that question.
- Writing as much information as you can that is at least tangential to the answer (this is recommended if you must attempt an answer to the question).

Index